JAGUAR XK120/XK140

Philip Porter

CONTENTS

Foulis

Haynes

A FOULIS Motoring Book

First published 1987

© **Haynes Publishing Group**

Published by:
Haynes Publishing Group,
Sparkford, Near Yeovil,
Somerset BA22 7JJ

Haynes Publications Inc.
861 Lawrence Drive, Newbury
Park, California 91320, USA

**British Library Cataloguing in
Publication Data**
Porter, Philip
    Jaguar XK120/XK140 super profile.—
(Super profile)
1. Jaguar automobile—History
I. Title II. Series
629.2'222   TL215.J3
ISBN 0-85429-573-9

**Library of Congress catalog
card number**
86-82632

Editor: Robert Iles
Series photographer: Andrew
Morland
Page layout: Peter Kay
Printed in England, by:
J.H. Haynes & Co. Ltd

Titles in the *Super Profile* series
Ariel Square Four (F388)
BMW R69 & R69S (F387)
Brough Superior SS100 (F365)
BSA A7 & A10 (F446)
BSA Bantam (F333)
BSA Gold Star (F483)
BSA M20 & M21 (F485)
Honda CB750 sohc (F351)
International Norton (F365)
KSS Velocette (F444)
Matchless G3L & G80 (F455)
MV Agusta America (F334)
Norton Commando (F335)
Norton International (F365)
Norton Manx (F452)
Sunbeam S7 & S8 (F363)
Triumph Thunderbird (F353)
Triumph Trident (F352)
Triumph Bonneville (F453)
Velocette KSS (F444)
Vincent Twins (F460)

AC/Ford/Shelby Cobra (F381)
Austin A30/A35 (F469)
*Austin-Healey 'Frogeye' Sprite
    (F343)*
Austin-Healey 100/4 (F487)
Chevrolet Corvette (F432)
*Datsun 240Z, 260Z and
    280Z (F488)*
Ferrari 250 GTO (F308)
Ferrari Daytona (F535)
Fiat X1/9 (F341)
*Ford 100E Anglia, Prefect &
    Popular (F470)*
*Ford Consul/Zephyr/Zodiac Mk 1
    (F497)*

*Ford Consul/Zephyr/Zodiac Mk 2
    (F531)*
Ford Cortina 1600E (F310)
Ford GT40 (F332)
Ginetta G15 (F496)
Jaguar E-Type (F370)
Jaguar D-Type & XKSS (F371)
Jaguar Mk 2 Saloons (F307)
Jaguar SS90 & SS100 (F372)
Lamborghini Countach (F553)
Lancia Stratos (F340)
Lotus Elan (F330)
Lotus Seven (F385)
MGB (F305)
*MG Midget & Austin-Healey
    Sprite (except 'Frogeye')
    (F344)*
Mini Cooper (F445)
Morris Minor Series MM (F412)
*Morris Minor & 1000 (ohv)
    (F331)*
Porsche 911 Carrera (F311)
Porsche 917 (F495)
Range Rover (F534)
Rolls-Royce Corniche (F411)
Triumph Stag (F342)
Triumph TR2/3/3A (F559)

Deltics (F430)
Great Western Kings (F426)
Gresley Pacifics (F429)
Intercity 125 (F428)
Royal Scots (F431)
V2 'Green Arrow' Class (F427)

Further titles in this series will be published at regular intervals. For information on new titles please contact your bookseller or write to the publisher.

FOREWORD

As is now well known, Jaguar only intended to produce something like 200 XK 120s and yet from this inauspicious beginning was born one of the greatest sports cars of all time. A car which would sell in thousands, would sire five Le Mans winners and put the Jaguar company on the world map, to say nothing of doing wonders for boosting British post-war prestige to new heights.

To properly appreciate what an enormous step forward the XK 120 was one must view it in the context of its introduction in 1948. Apart from the B.M.W. 328 and the occasional exotic Italian creation, all enveloping bodies for sports cars were still a thing of the future. Furthermore the performance of which the 120 was capable was only achieved by racing cars. That this is true is evidenced by the fact that a largely standard 120 was unlucky not to finish the 1950 Le Mans race in third place or even higher.

For such a car, with racing car performance, to have the ride of a saloon was equally unheard of. The roadholding was as impressive and the new engine smooth, powerful, glamorous in appearance and technically advanced. It is history that this engine was to become a legend. In its next 38 years, presuming that production will cease with the introduction of the XJ40 saloon, it would power increasingly powerful sports cars, large luxury saloons, small sporting saloons, Dennis fire-engines, Alvis tanks, the five Le Mans winners mentioned, innumerable other successful sports racing cars and, finally, the XJ saloons which seriously challenged that august maker of the finest motor cars, Rolls Royce.

As if this great list were not enough, it can be stated that in each of the above mentioned roles the XK engine distinguished itself. The Mark VIIs won races and rallies, whilst the Mark Is and IIs made that dominance supreme. The sensational E-type with its (almost) 150 mph performance set yet new standards and was greeted with the same sort of acclamation and adulation as the XK 120, thirteen years before it.

The famous and charismatic C-type and D-types were, of course, XK powered and the ridiculous prices examples fetch today is some sort of measure of the esteem in which they are held. More importantly they are revered, almost worshipped, by enthusiasts. Second only to that reverence and enthusiasm is that held for the XK's themselves. The depth of enthusiasm in the XK Register section of the Jaguar Drivers' Club is testament to that.

And all this furore, all these achievements, all the publicity began with the XK 120.

But that it not all. The exciting new 120 was not just a magnificent engine. It had startling good looks and a well designed chassis that contributed much to the ride and cornering ability. It was practical in spite of its performance and, in true Lyons tradition, the modest price met with utter incomprehension.

Demand completely outstripped supply and, as and when examples became available, they proceeded to record a prodigious number of wins in sporting events of all natures in all parts of the world. Not least of these countries was the United States which took to the XK 120 like the proverbial duck taking to water.

A high proportion was exported and one American of some fame, writing in 1950, summed up the regard in which the transatlantic sportsman held the new XK. "A masterpiece of design and construction for a production car." Clark Gable was just one of the many illustrious owners of XKs.

In the early fifties Jaguar broadened the appeal of the 120 by introducing first a Fixed Head and then a Drophead version. These more refined models succeeded in introducing yet more owners to the joys of XK motoring.

The XK 140 which followed the 120 is not always held in quite such high esteem. In my opinion this is wrong. Admittedly in looks the 140 was a slight dilution of the original clean classic lines with its over-heavy bumpers and grille, but in many other respects the successor was superior. The steering was more pleasant, the handling a little improved and the engine was blessed with a touch more power.

It will not have escaped the reader's notice that I write of the XKs with some enthusiasm. I have been lucky enough to own examples of each model, albeit most requiring extensive restoration! I acquired these cars many years ago before the inflated prices of today and I mention the fact simply to illustrate that I am not biased for or against any particular model. I must say, though, that I have used my XK 140 Roadster on and off for the last 12 years and no car has ever given me more pleasure.

I cannot help reflecting that the XK story is a perfect tribute to Sir William Lyons and Mr. Heynes plus his team. It was Sir William who had the nerve and imagination to lay down the criteria, insisted on the twin-cam engine and designed the stunning body. It was Bill Heynes, together with his colleagues, Baily, Hassan and others, who translated the criteria so brilliantly into reality.

The XK story is a microcosm of the Jaguar tale, and as such is a fitting monument to those great individualists.

I should like to acknowledge my debt of gratitude to John Bridcutt, Andrew Morland, Roger Clinkscales, Barry Williams, Vic Gill, Bob Davis, Mike Barker, Harry Phillips, Phil Weaver and Norman Dewis.

Philip Porter

HISTORY

From the very beginning Swallow sidecars and cars, and later SS and SS Jaguars had all been of sporting appearance. With the advent of the "100" model the performance began to match the looks and these machines enjoyed some competition success. Further developments were inevitably interrupted by the war and in their first pre-war literature the newly named Jaguar Cars Limited stated the following. "Although illustrations and descriptions of the Drophead coupe and the Open '100' Model are included in this abridged catalogue, no delivery dates can be given for these models as production will for some time be concentrated on saloon models only."

The "100" was, in fact, never to be put into production again. However during the war William Lyons (he was not to become Sir William until 1956) organised the factory fire watching rota so that he, his Chief Engineer, Bill Heynes, Claude Baily and Wally Hassan should share such duties on a Sunday evening from 6 p.m. During these sessions they would discuss future plans and Lyons outlined his ideas. Above all they used the time to discuss the new engines that Lyons felt would be needed to see off the competition.

Thus were the first outlines for the new engines which would power a new range of saloons drawn up. Pre-war the company had used Standard engines, but Lyons felt that his company should become independent of an outside firm and furthermore that he required units which were more advanced, more refined and more powerful. Ever thinking of style, he stressed to his engineers that the engine must be a glamorous one, both in specification and appearance. The idea of a twin overhead cam unit appealed to him from the start.

Discussions at first centred around a six cylinder power unit of $2^{1}/_{2}$ litres. Fears of post-war restrictions on fuel and high vehicle taxation led the team to believe initially that anything larger might not be practical. A smaller four cylinder engine sharing certain measurements to enable manufacture on common machinery was also envisaged and in fact the first to be built.

The different designs were codenamed and the first five, XA to XE were not actually built. The first to exist was named XF and was a twin cam unit of 1,360 cc with hemispherical combustion chambers. Cylinder block strength and crankshaft durability were found to be lacking and so XG was built. This one was based on the 1,776 cc Standard unit and followed B.M.W. practice having valves operated from a single side camshaft in the cylinder block. Two examples were built.

However noisy valve gear precluded this design and the 2 litre four cylinder XJ was built. This proved to be very close to the final design. Harry Weslake was retained to advise on cylinder head and manifold design. A six cylinder of 3,182 cc was constructed incorporating all the development carried out on the smaller engine. The only snag was a lack of torque and so the stroke was increased from 98 mm to 106 mm, which together with a bore of 83 mm gave the final dimensions (3,442 cc) of what became known as the "XK'.

In fact there were Mark I, II and III versions of the XK unit built between '46 and '49 and several 2 litre, 3.2 and 3.4 engines were built. They were subjected to considerable testing over the period.

Meanwhile development had been continuing apace on chassis design and independent front suspension. With regard to the latter, Heynes had always admired the Citroen system and similarly used a torsion bar as the springing medium. Stress was reduced by a good length of bar and ball-pins were adopted for the suspension joints.

All this work was carried out for the new saloon car, but for various reasons the body would not be ready in 1948, yet the new engine, chassis and front suspension were. The stop-gap saloons were therefore replaced by the evolutionary Mark V which had the new chassis and independent front suspension. However it was felt that it would be wrong to introduce the exciting new engine in what was basically an old design a little updated. It was decided to hold it back for the Mark VII.

However Jaguar had a high performance engine raring to go and no sports car. How ideal it would be to offer a limited number of sports cars which would attract some welcome publicity and allow the car to "try out" the new engines on customers who being sporting types would be rather more tolerant of any little problems, if any there should be. The idea was to offer both the smaller and larger engines.

Thus the XK 120 was born and the XK 100 was still-born. Lyons, as was his wont, had been playing around with designs even during the war. Indeed he had found a little time to build several half-bodies, split down the centre line, with employees Fred Gardner and Cyril Holland. Having taken the decision to produce a sports car he had only a matter of months to design a body to clothe a shortened Mark V chassis in time for its debut at the 1948 Motor Show.

The XK 120

The car which shared the stand with the new saloon was barely ready in time and in fact varied from production cars in various details. It was entitled the XK 120, the numbers suggesting the car's capability in miles per hour. The intended XK 100, which would have had the four cylinder engine, was mentioned in advance publicity and the first brochure, but did not appear.

It has been suggested to me recently by two sources that the car was about four inches shorter and Lyons decided very much at the last minute that it did not look right. A blue car is recalled being around the factory for several years. However this recollection conflicts with the quoted dimensions of the "100" which were identical to the "120".

There is no doubt that an XK 100 was built and indeed it was still on the list of Experimental Cars held as late as 1953. At some stage it was broken up.

A number of other reasons have been offered over the years for the non-appearance of the XK 100 including that the tooling could not easily be shared as planned, and simply that demand was so great for the "six" that there was no reason to produce the smaller brother. Wally Hassan recalls there were problems with secondary vibrations when the "four" was fitted in a car.

Some months before the launch an example of the XK "four" had been lent to the speed record specialist, Lt. Col. Goldie Gardner to fit in his normally MG

engined record breaker EX135. With a race tuned Jaguar unit he broke three International Class E records achieving 176.694 mph. This was an excellent foretaste of things to come.

This engine has always been referred to in the past as an XJ unit, but it was in fact an XK. The capacity was 1970 cc and it had a compression ratio of no less than 13.57:1. A number of different carburettor set-ups were tried, but with the most successful, two S.U.s, it produced 142 bhp.

The reaction to the XK 120's debut at Earls Court was amazement from Press and public alike though there was a scattering of sceptics. However they would soon be silenced when the 120 showed that for once the advertising men were not getting carried away with the exuberance of their own verbosity.

The brochure almost played down the performance majoring on the civilised aspects of the car, indeed the XK might very aptly be christened "the first civilised sports car". The brochure ran, "whilst the Type XK Jaguar '120' Super Sports Model has been designed with every consideration directed to performance, its appearance and comfort are of the highest order. Perfect streamlining combined with sweeping contours endow this car with a beauty and distinction seldom found in high performance sports models. The generous width of the cockpit (52 inches) and the deep, resilient upholstery afford perfect comfort, whilst complete weather protection is provided by hood and side curtains which are stowed out of sight when not in use".

The Show car did not, in fact, as has always been assumed, have the 3.4 engine, but had a 3.2 litre unit. It is almost certain the car had not even run prior to the Show, certainly not outside the factory. When it was first run it proved to be rather disappointing and could not approach the magic 120.

Sutton, the Test Driver, in his report of 10th December, 1948 described 'Test 1' rather quaintly as 'short run up Keresley Road'. The next test consisted of 'running the car' and the third was described as, 'tests up to maximum speeds'. The best achieved was just 106 mph and Sutton commented, 'this speed is obviously low'.

In true Jaguar tradition a long development period followed which explains why none were sold or available for demonstration for several months. Indeed on 17th March, 1949 Wally Hassan filed a report entitled, 'Points requiring design or improvement before release for customers or demonstration purposes'.

Owing to the limited production run the bodies were hand-made in aluminium by an outside supplier, Messrs. J.H. Cooke & Sons of Nottingham. The front bulkhead was of steel and the rear bodywork was affixed to a laminated ash frame. The front and rear sections were joined by internal sills of steel and wood construction. Inner panels such as the boot structure and inner wings were of steel and the floors plywood. Removable spats enclosed the rear wings and the windscreen was detachable to allow the fitting of aero screens. The spare wheel was carried in the boot beneath a removable plywood floor and behind the 14 gallon petrol tank.

Most of the Press were surprised by the announcement of the new sports car at the Motor Show. When announcing the new saloons just prior to the annual extravaganza, Lyons referred in his speech on September 30th to his intention to again produce a sports car. What the journalists did not expect was to actually see a new car, a radical new car at that, just a few weeks later.

Whilst their breath might have been taken away, their ability to express lavish praise in print had not left them. The acclamation was instant and genuine, especially remembering the tendency to understatement in those days. "The Motor" complimented the coachwork describing it as "thoroughly post-war and extremely attractive in a way at once satisfying to the modernists and acceptable to those of more conservative tastes". They drew attention to "the exceptionally high power/weight ratio of 145 b.h.p. per ton".

"The Autocar" began their first report with the words, "there is an exciting new Jaguar to thrill the fast-motoring fans". The writer explained that, "the new XK engines have been designed to incorporate the most advanced yet well-proved points of technical knowledge". In a further article a few weeks later the magazine offered their approval of Lyons' body design and described the oft-praised purity of line in a novel expression. "Designed," they wrote, "to offer minimum air resistance, the body is streamlined from end to end and is devoid of excrescences."

J. Eason Gibson, writing in "Country Life" no less, showed commendable foresight and exuded enthusiasm. "One of the most admirable cars," he stated, "is certainly the new Sports Jaguar. Apart from its technical features ... this car reaches a standard of functional beauty never before achieved by a British manufacturer. As a prestige earner abroad it is probably the most important new car to be shown by the British Industry."

With this acclaim being translated into firm orders, Jaguar realised there was no way they were going to be able to cope with the demand, certainly with the chosen method of construction. So the decision was taken actually during the Show to tool-up for pressed steel panels. Deliveries, even in aluminium form, did not commence until July, 1949 and the first steel cars were not delivered until the following April. The total number of "ali-120s", as they are often known today, was 240.

If there were any doubts about the manufacturer's claims for the performance of the 120, these were dispelled by two events.

Firstly in late May, Lyons chartered a Dakota and flew a party of journalists out to Belgium where Ron "Soapy" Sutton proceeded to demonstrate what a carefully prepared XK 120 was capable of. Using a stretch of the Jabbeke-Aeltre motorway he achieved, with the optional undershield fitted, an officially timed mean of 126.448 mph. With a small cowl replacing the windscreen and metal tonneau cover over the passenger area, he recorded a mean of 132.596 mph and then pottered past the journalists again at 10 mph in top!

'Californian Autonews' commented that, "it is typically British that Jaguars never claimed more than 120 mph for this car". That British institution, 'The Times' proclaimed, "the speed achieved is so far ahead of current sports car performance that it represents a major achievement by the British Motor Industry".

'Autocar' expressed the view that, "Jaguar have established their car as the world's fastest unsupercharged catalogue model with full touring body work. Indeed it is very doubtful whether any standard model in catalogue condition, even with the aid of a supercharger, has ever recorded such speeds". 'Sporting Life' proffered the opinion that, "never has a more impressive demonstration of silent effortless speed been given". Tom Wisdom, no stranger to fast cars, summed up the XK 120 admirably when he wrote in the 'Daily Herald', "it is the fastest ever tourer, yet as docile in heavy traffic as the most expensive and biggest saloon".

As if to underline the point an excellent opportunity to test the XK's racing prowess presented itself when the BRDC announced that a Production Car Race would be held in August, 1949 at Silverstone. After a private practice session to convince Lyons of the car's capability of winning, three 120s painted individually red, white and blue were lent to distinguished drivers to enter.

Prince Bira was leading when he spun off due to a puncture caused by the inadvertent fitting of a touring tube, but Leslie Johnson and Peter Walker gave a convincing performance taking the first two places. Such demonstrations as Jabbeke and Silverstone only served to make the already long waiting list even longer.

Early in 1950 the factory supplied six aluminium cars to selected amateurs including Johnson, Walker, Tom Wisdom, Clemente Biondetti and Ian Appleyard. These virtual 'works' cars were used widely and most successfully. Johnson with JWK 651 finished fifth in the Mille Miglia and three cars were entered for Le Mans. Entering merely as an experiment and with no thoughts of success, the cars surprised everyone including Jaguar. After 21 hours Johnson was in third position and catching the leaders when the clutch went. The other two cars finished in 12th and 15th positions.

For the Tourist Trophy at Dundrod in September, Wisdom lent his car to a young man called Stirling Moss who was going indecently quickly in 500s. Moss did his reputation and career a deal of good that day when, in appalling conditions, he trounced the opposition to record a famous win. As if to emphasise the point on his last lap in torrential rain and growing gloom, he set a new lap record!

Ian Appleyard already successful in rallying with an SS 100 replaced the car with one of the 'factory' 120s. The car's registration, NUB 120, was to become famous as he clocked up a prodigious number of successes. In the 1950 Alpine Rally he took a class win and a Coupe des Alpes for a penalty-free run. The following year saw victory in the Tulip, Morecombe, RAC, and London Rallies plus another Coupe des Alpes in the Alpine.

At the Geneva Motor Show in March, Jaguar unveiled the XK 120 Fixed Head. Reminiscent of pre-war Bugattis the Fixed Head was another Lyons success with the roof blending beautifully into the basic roadster shape.

This was a more sophisticated XK retaining all the performance of the open model yet with extra refinements. The interior was lavishly appointed with figured walnut facia and door cappings, wind-up windows, veneered instrument panel, and improved heating. The Fixed Head was a true Grand Touring car and ideal for long continental journeys. Moss used one for this very purpose and told me some years ago he found it an ideal, long-legged car for rapid travel. He even used his for towing a caravan at times!

A prototype Fixed Head was certainly built and running in mid-1950, but it differed from the final production car in a number of details. Chassis number one, right-hand drive was actually fitted with the 2 litre engine, but after a period in the Experimental Department was dismantled. The second was retained by Experimental and, registered LWK 707, used by Bill Heynes. The third, which I have owned for many years, was not despatched till January 1953, indicating that the vast majority were exported.

Indeed only 195 right-hand drive Fixed Heads were ever built making them a very rare car today, a fact that is not always realised.

Fixed Heads had moulded-in sidelights painted body colour rather than the separate chrome items and this alteration was adopted on the Open cars in October, 1952. With the advent of the closed car, footwell ventilators were adopted on both models.

Following the excellent showing the 120s gave at Le Mans in 1950, it was decided to build a car specifically for the race in 1951. Three examples of the car which the factory always referred to as the XK 120C were entered and Walker and Whitehead brought their machine home in first place. This was to be the beginning of a long and distinguished competition career for the company, particularly at the famous and publicity-rich French classic.

Developed for, and as a result of, the racing C-types and 'factory' XKs, the company introduced a range of tuning items. These included 8:1 and 9:1 pistons, camshafts with $3/8''$ lift as opposed to the standard $5/16''$, a twin exhaust system, lightened flywheel, crankshaft damper, thicker rear spring leaves, uprated torsion bars and a more suitable clutch. Apart from mechanical items a full length undershield, aeroscreens, cowlings for the mirror and aeroscreens, and bucket seats, which must have been a great improvement over the standard bench seats when cornering enthusiastically, completed the options.

Coinciding with the introduction of the Fixed Head, Jaguar offered Special Equipment versions of both open and closed 120s. These cars, known in the States as the XK 120M, featured the high-lift cams, crankshaft damper, wire spoke wheels with splined hubs and "knock-on hub caps", a dual exhaust system and stiffer 1'' torsion bars.

In 1951 the competition successes continued with Moss winning at Silverstone, Johnny Claes posting the only penalty-free run ever on the arduous Liege-Rome-Liege Rally and the same pilot winning a production car race at Spa. Towards the end of the year Ecurie Ecosse was formed around a team of three XK 120s.

In 1952 the Fixed Head, LWK 707, mentioned above, made the headlines when driven by Johnson, Moss, Fairman and Hadley around the French Montlhery track for seven days and nights non-stop. The Jaguar was driven for over 168 hours at over 100 mph. In covering 16,851.73 miles, the 120 broke four World and Class records and one Class record.

Following the run the engine was stripped for examination and found to be in excellent condition. The technical report stated that, "the crankshaft was still within production tolerances and would have been passed by the inspection department for installation in a new car".

The Drophead Coupe model was introduced in April, 1953. This was a halfway house model between the roadster with its crude hood and sidescreens, and the grand touring Fixed Head. The Drophead shared many of the features of the latter apart from the fact that it had, obviously, a folding hood. This hood was a rather posh lined affair with a rear window which could be unzipped. Mechanically the Dropheads were identical to the other 120s apart from the use of Salisbury back axles which were being gradually adopted on all models from '52.

Amongst other items offered to improve performance, a new cylinder head was available in small quantities coinciding with the Drophead's debut. The C-type head, as it was called, was obviously based on the design used for the racing cars. The exhaust valve diameter was

Super Profile

increased from 1⁷/16'' to 1⁵/8'' and the inlet and exhaust porting was increased in size. An improved manifold and 2'' SU carburettors were also offered. With the standard manifold and carbs, the 'C' headed engine developed 210 bhp as opposed to the Special Equipment car's 190.

In October, 1953 a couple of cars were taken out to Jabbeke in Belgium. One was a rather special XK 120. A metal tonneau covered the cockpit and a perspex bubble was fitted to this. The bumpers and lights had been removed and the grille partially covered. A modified engine and 2.92:1 axle had been fitted and Norman Dewis, the Chief Test Driver, proceeded to achieve the quite remarkable officially timed speed of 172.412 mph!

Development had been continuing at the factory with experimental Mark II and Mark III versions of the 120 built incorporating a number of new features. In late '52 a Mark IV coupe was built and this had many of the modifications of the next model.

Leading up to the 1954 Motor Show, production of the XK120s was gradually phased out in time for the introduction of its successor, the evolutionary XK 140.

The XK140

From introduction all three models were offered. They differed from the 120s in a number of details rather than radical development. The grille was now a cast item and the rather dainty 120 bumpers and overriders were replaced by a one-piece hefty bumper on the front and hefty quarter bumpers on the rear to satisfy American requirements. The 'tripod' headlamps were succeeded by 'J' type ones, the front wings sprouted flasher lamps, the rear

lamps were a little different and the bonnet and bootlid now had chrome strips. That on the bootlid contained a badge commemorating the Le Mans victories. The bootlid no longer continued to the extremity of the tail and a panel below carried the number plate. The arrangement of boot area and spare wheel was somewhat altered.

Of rather more importance, the engine was moved some three inches forward. This was done to increase legroom, but had the additional advantage of improving the roadholding. The 140s were fitted with the 190 bhp S.E. engine as standard, the uprated torsion bars and the former recirculating ball type steering was superseded by rack and pinion. Telescopic shockers replaced the rear lever type of the earlier cars. Special Equipment cars now had wire wheels and Lucas foglamps. The 210 bhp C-type headed versions were fitted with dual exhaust systems. With a little more power and despite the extra weight the 140s were slightly faster than their predecessors.

The Open 2-seater was otherwise little changed. It and the Drophead no longer had two six-volt batteries, but instead were fitted with one twelve-volt mounted not behind the seats as previously, but in the nearside front wing. The Drophead and Fixed Heads were given the benefit of two small rear seats for two children or an occasional adult.

The Drophead can be distinguished from its predecessor by the adoption of a larger rear window and the Fixed Head was rather more altered than the other two. The windscreen line was moved forward a little and the rear extended some 6¹/2'' farther back. With the bulkhead modified so that the footwells projected either side of the engine, the front seats were moved about twelve inches forward and the XK 140 Fixed Head was a considerably roomier

car. The lever type door handles were succeeded by plunger types.

The option of overdrive, and later automatic transmission, contributed to the 140's grand touring image. In the States, where the brochure claimed owners would, "enjoy Jaguar's classic, sculptured beauty that excites envy wherever you drive," the S.E. model was described as the 'M' and the C-type headed version as the 'MC'. The models were known as the "Roadster – 2-seater with all-weather body, the Coupe – 2/3-seater and the Convertible – 2-seater plus seats for two children".

The XK 140s continued to enjoy the same success as the 120s and remained very popular in the States. In competition the 140 was less successful being at a disadvantage with its greater weight. Furthermore sports car racing had evolved into a more specialised and serious affair with specially designed cars for competition, a trend that Jaguar themselves had influenced with the C-types and D-types.

However several 140s distinguished themselves in events. Perhaps the best known was the lone 140 F.H.C. entered by privateers Bolton and Walshaw in the 1956 Le Mans race. They were surprisingly well-placed in 12th position when the French organisers, incorrectly it now transpires, disqualified the car with just a few hours to go for allegedly taking on fuel a lap early.

The same year Ian Appleyard, though officially retired, used his 140 F.H.C., VUB 140, to take second place in the R.A.C. Rally and Guyot won his class in a 2-seater in the Mille Miglia. Whilst 140s enjoyed occasional and modest success in rallies over the years, their appearance on race tracks was even more infrequent. One or two enjoyed some success in the States but in Europe there were few classes that catered for them and the poor old brakes were really not up to it. Curiously one of the most successful racing 140s was campaigned as late as the sixties. It was driven by David Hobbs and fitted with disc brakes and the Hobbs Mechamatic transmission.

Production of the XK140s continued until February, 1957 when they were superseded by

another evolutionary model, the XK 150. Whilst the concept of the 150 was similar to the original 120s, that concept was considerably updated with such important features as disc brakes.

The XK 150 was in many ways a very different car and will be the subject of a future 'Super Profile'.

EVOLUTION

Evolution

January 1950: Engine oil level – Service Bulletin No. 58 stated, ''Some complaints have been received of oil cavitation taking place on rapid acceleration when the oil is cold causing loss of oil pressure.

It has been decided to revise the engine oil level and it is requested that all distributors check and amend the dipstick oil level marking as follows.

On cars issued to date the distance between the underside of the collar on the dipstick, in which a felt washer is fitted and which meets up with the crankcase when the stick is in position, to the high level mark on the dipstick is $8^{11}/16''$ (221 mm) and a new high level mark should be cut on the dipstick $5/8''$ (16 mm) above the original mark, making the measurement between the underside of the collar and the new high level mark $8^1/16''$ (205 mm).

It should be noted that with the new engine oil level the total oil capacity of the engine now becomes 29 Imperial pints (28.8 U.S. pints) (13.6 litres).

It will thus be noted that 5 Imperial pints of oil are contained in the oil filter, crankshaft oilways, etc.

Owners should be advised that the oil level should not be allowed to drop below the second mark (the old high level mark) on the dipstick.''

Timing gauge (part no. C.3993) included in toolkit.

Steering track rod bearings – Service Bulletin No. 61 stated, ''The thread bearings at either end of the track rod ... are being replaced by rubber bearings on cars being produced. These rubber bearings require no maintenance and should not in any circumstances be lubricated. The lubricating nipples previously situated at the track rod ends are consequently no longer fitted.''

April 1950: Throttle restrictor – Service Bulletin No. 66 stated, ''To prevent cars being run at an excessive speed during their early life it has been considered advisable to restrict the throttle opening by the fitting of a stop on the underside of the accelerator pedal.

This stop is secured to the pedal by a setscrew which is in turn locked by a wire and lead seal. The stop is to be removed at the time the first service is carried out, that is, after the first 750 miles.''

Front brake air scoops. The same Bulletin stated, ''To prevent the possibility of dirt or water getting into the front brakes through the air scoops, two blanking plates, Part No. C.4292, will in future be issued with each car to be fitted, when considered necessary, in place of the normal stone guard, Part No. C.3527.

The brake air scoops are fitted to avoid the possibility of brake fade when cars are driven at maximum speed and the brakes are used to the maximum degree.

It is suggested that the blanking plates should be fitted where the cars are operated only at reasonable speeds and where dirty road conditions, or persistently wet weather, exist.''

July 1950: To eradicate low speed steering wobble, a new Ferobestos socket was adopted for the lower wishbone ball assembly. A plug replaced the greaser.

August 1950: Front suspension – Service Bulletin No. 70 stated, ''the castor angle on the XK 120 chassis has been altered from 5° positive to 3° positive on the following chassis numbers and subsequent: 670439 OTS LHD & 660126 OTS RHD.''

Newton Shock absorbers – ''Reference to the use of S.A. 10 engine oil in the Operating and Maintenance Handbook should be deleted and the following recommendations are now given:- Mobil Shock Absorber Oil Light, Castrol Shockol, Shell Donax A.1., Esso Shock Absorber Oil, and Prices' Energol S.A. Light.''

Fitment of air cleaners – Service Bulletin No. 71 stated, ''the fitment of individual air cleaners to the carburetters ... has now been standardised.

It is also considered desirable that they should be fitted to cars already delivered and not so fitted. Air cleaners will be supplied on a 'free of charge' basis ... '' Parts required: LHD C.4496 Air Cleaner Assy Qty 2, C.4475 Gaskets Qty 2, FS.105/6D Setscrew Qty 4, FG.105/X Washer for setscrew Qty 4. RHD as above except C.4496 Front Air Cleaner Assy Qty 1, C.4732 Rear Air Cleaner Assy Qty 1. Hydraulic brake fluid reservoir to be repositioned by moving approximately 2" to the rear.

December 1950: Filler plug deleted on Newton front shock absorbers.

Brake shoe rattle – rear brakes only – Service Bulletin No. 73 stated, ''if complaints of rattle at the rear of the car are received check by noting if the rattle is eliminated when the handbrake is lightly applied.

Rattle can be caused by the rear brake shoes butting against the back plate on rough surfaces. The fitting of beehive springs located through the rear brake shoes to the brackets on the brakes back plate effects a cure."

·Part No. 21686 Beehive Spring Qty 4, 21728 Bracket Qty 4.

Valve clearance adjustment pads – Service Bulletin No. 74 stated, "the range of adjustment pads or biscuits has now been increased and the method of identification revised as follows:

Parts Nos. C.2243/1 – 19 now represent a thickness range from 0.085" to 0.105". The original numerical markings have been superseded by alphabetical markings from A to S inclusive."

January 1951: Brake linings – Service Bulletin No. 89 stated, "a change in the type of brake lining has been introduced on the following chassis numbers: RHD 660551 and future, LHD 671097 and future.

The linings now used are Mintex M.14, these linings having a lower co-efficient of friction than the Mintex M.15 lining fitted on earlier cars.

When M.14 linings are fitted in place of M.15 it will be found that the amount of pedal pressure required to operate the brakes is somewhat greater than previously and if certain customers, for example lady drivers, should desire lighter operation of the foot brake, this can be achieved in the following manner". There follows a description of re-drilling the brake pedal to take the master cylinder push rod yoke clevis pin to 2⅝" from the brake pedal fulcrum.

March 1951: Modifications introduced that affected interchangeability of E.N.V. rear axles.

November 1951: Cylinder block heater adaptor – Service Bulletin No. 97 stated, "note that on XK 120 engines, Engine No. W.3686 and future ... and certain individual engines prior to this number, a boss is incorporated in the cylinder block casting at the rear left side of the engine above

and slightly forward of the oil sump dipstick, this boss being fitted with an internal hexagon plug, being tapped 1" American standard pipe thread for fitment of a U.S. standard engine heater element No. 7, manufactured by The Electric Heating & Manufacturing Co. Ltd., when so desired."

Footwell ventilators fitted in front wings from chassis nos. 660675 and 671097.

Certain changes effected in connecting rod design, rods still interchangeable in sets.

Air conditioning installation – from Chassis no. 660911 and 671493 an air conditioner unit without demisting or defrosting of the windscreen fitted as standard.

Engine oil sump – "from Engine No. W.3593 to 3596 inclusive, and from W.3635 and onwards, the Mark VII type stepped sump is fitted and oil capacity amended as follows:

	British Imperial	U.S.	Litres
Engine sump	21 pints	25 pints	12 litres
Engine total	24 pints	28 pints	13.5 litres

February 1952: Revised timing chain tensioner adopted (from W.4052).

Rear Axle – Certain cars after the following chassis numbers:
OTS RHD 660935
FHC RHD 669003
OTS LHD 671797
FHC LHD 679222
are fitted with Salisbury axles of 3.77:1 ratio. These axles can be easily distinguished from the E.N.V. type axles in that they have a non-detachable nose piece and that the filler plug is situated in the cover at the rear of the axle casing.

Gearbox – from chassis numbers:-
OTS RHD 660935
FHC RHD 669003
OTS LHD 671797
FHC LHD 679215

and onwards, a short main shaft gearbox without a rear extension has been introduced. With this modification a longer propeller shaft and a speedometer cable of different length are fitted.

April 1952: Service Bulletin No. 105 – Valve guides altered to fit ⅜" camshaft without additional modification (from W.4483).

Gearbox – "due to supply difficulties it has been found necessary in some instances, to revert to the fitting of the long mainshaft gearbox (prefix letter SH or JH).

Oil filter assembly (C.4767) adopted (from W.4383).

Front brakes – From chassis numbers:
OTS RHD 660980
FHC RHD 669003
OTS LHD 672049
FHC LHD 679622
"and onwards, cars are fitted with self-adjusting front brakes, and a tandem type master cylinder fed by a divided fluid supply tank. A different type of rear brake adjuster is also fitted."

May 1952: Wheel rim width (pressed steel wheels) increased from 5" to 5½".

Integral fan pulley and hub and 6-bladed fan adopted (from W.5465).

June 1952: Shock absorbers, front – from chassis numbers: as front brakes above, Newton telescopic shock absorbers Part No. C.7183 with revised valve settings fitted.

October 1952: Sump oil level indicator and element not fitted (from W.6149). Blanking plate fitted.

Altered gearbox top cover (C.6878) and reverse striking rod fitted (from JL.13154).

Modification to auxiliary starting carburettor switch-plunger. Moulded in sidelights adopted (as FHC) from 661025 and 672963. Demister vents fitted for windscreen from 661026 and 672963.

December 1952: 1st and

2nd synchronising sleeve fitted with stop pin (from JL.13834/SL6313A).

Special Equipment rear springs (C.5721) adopted as standard from:

OTS RHD 661040
FHC RHD 669003
OTS LHD 673320
FHC LHD 679222

Vacuum operated Trico windscreen washer introduced.

For access to front prop shaft UJ and grease nipples, removable plate adopted on right of transmission tunnel.

January 1953: OTS hood rear window unzippable from 661046 and 673396.

February 1953: Fixed Head – RF needles replaced by W.O.2.

March 1953: Modified water pump (from W.7207).

Special Equipment Fixed Head – single exhaust system (from RHD 669005 & LHD 680738).

April 1953: 4HA axle (3.54) fitted as standard from:

OTS RHD 661054
FHC RHD 669185
DHC RHD 667271
OTS LHD 673695
FHC LHD 680880
DHC LHD 677016

May 1953: Cast-iron crankshaft damper superseded by malleable-iron item (W.8381).

Special Equipment lightened flywheel adopted on all models (from W.8275).

June 1953: Revised con-rods with increased length cap bolt bosses (from W.8643).

Mintex M.20 brake linings adopted.

Modified speedometer cable adopted.

August 1953: Suppressors adopted on all models.

September 1953: Uprated change-speed forks (from JL.18457/SL.9984A).

Altered tappet settings for engines fitted with 3/8" cams.

November 1953: Commencement of F.1001 engine number series.

January 1954: Altered tappet settings for all models (004 inlet/006 exhaust, competition cars – 006 inlet/010 exhaust).

Altered cigar lighter adopted.

April 1954: Revised inlet valve with depression in cylinder head.

Altered exhaust valves and shortened guides (from F.2421).

May 1954: Revised timing chain tensioner, plated with hard chrome for improved wear and polished (from F.2773).

August 1954: Two rear reflectors fitted either side of number plate.

September 1954: Different handbrake lever adopted from:

OTS RHD 661170
FHC RHD 669185
DHC RHD 667271
OTS LHD 675763
FHC LHD 681471
DHC LHD 678390

140 type flat horn push (C.5558) adopted from:

OTS RHD 661172
FHC RHD 669194
DHC RHD 667280
OTS LHD 675926
FHC LHD 681481
DHC LHD 678418

XK 140

February 1955: Circular front crank seal, rotor type oil pump and pressure relief valve in filter head fitted (from G.1908).

June 1955: Altered rear wheel cylinders adopted.

Overdrive relay adopted from:
OTS RHD 800031
FHC RHD 804121
DHC RHD 807113
OTS LHD 811382
FHC LHD 814216
DHC LHD 817426

September 1955: Castor angle altered to $1^1/2 - 2$ degrees positive from $2^1/2 - 3$, to minimise kick-back.

Spring bladed lower timing chain tensioner superseded by Renolds hydraulic spring loaded type with cylinder block modified to provide lubrication from tensioner to chain.

December 1955: Shorter studs used on cylinder head inlet side (from G.6233), different oil filter cannister (from G.6233) and overdrive throttle switch adopted.

April 1956: Rear axle fitted with larger sized drive gear bolts.

Different exhaust valves and guides (as C-type) adopted (from G.6678.S).

Modified rings fitted (from G.7229).

September 1956: Fly-off type handbrake lever adopted from:

OTS RHD 800072
FHC RHD 804767
DHC RHD 807441
OTS LHD 812647
FHC LHD 815755
DHC LHD 818729

October 1956: Doors on FHC and DHC now manufactured from steel rather than aluminium from:

FHC RHD 804781
DHC RHD 807447
FHC LHD 815773
DHC LHD 818796

February 1957: Steel head gasket adopted.

January 1958: (after demise of 140) Brake servo kit offered.

SPECIFICATION

XK 120

Models	Open Two-Seater Super Sports (Roadster), Fixed-Head Coupe, Drophead Coupe.
Built	Foleshill, Coventry until 1951, then Browns Lane, Allesley, Coventry.
Period current	OTS 1948 – 1954 (available from '49) FHC 1951 – 1954 DHC 1953 – 1954

Chassis Numbers

	RHD	LHD	
OTS From	660001	670001	("S" prefix indicates
FHC	669001	679001	Special Equipment)
DHC	667001	677001	

Drive Configuration Front engine, rear wheel drive.

Numbers Manufactured

	OTS	FHC	DHC
RHD	1175	195	294
LHD	6437	2484	1471

Engine Six cylinder 3^1/$_2$ litre Jaguar XK engine, 70° twin overhead camshafts driven by two-stage duplex roller chain; 83 mm bore x 106 mm stroke; 3,442 cc developing 160 bhp at 5,000 rpm; directly operated valves and austenetic cast iron seats; compression ratio 8:1 (7:1 & 9:1 optional); high grade chrome iron cylinder block; cylinder head of high tensile aluminium alloy with spherical combustion chambers; aluminium alloy pistons; twin S.U. carburettors with electrically controlled automatic choke; 2^3/$_4$'' diameter counterweighted crankshaft carried in 7 large steel backed precision bearings. Maximum torque 1951 lbs ft at 2,500 rpm.
Special Equipment engine 180 bhp at 5,300 rpm

Chassis Straight plane steel box section frame of immense strength. Torsional rigidity ensured by large box section cross members.

Transmission	Four speed single helical synchromesh gearbox. Synchromesh on 2nd, 3rd and top. Gear ratios: early cars 1st and reverse 12.29; 2nd 7.22; 3rd 4.98; later cars 1st and reverse 11.95; 2nd 7.01; 3rd 4.84: axle ratios ENV 3.27, 3.64, 3.92, 4.30; Salisbury 3.27, 3.54, 3.77, 4.09
Suspension	Independent front suspension incorporating transverse wishbones and long torsion bars with Newton telescopic type hydraulic shock absorbers. Rear suspension by long silico-manganese steel half elliptic springs controlled by Girling PV.7 hydraulic shock absorbers. Front anti-roll bar.
Brakes	Lockheed full hydraulic two-leading-shoe front and 12″ drums, friction lining area 208 sq ins. Central fly-off handbrake operating on the rear wheels only.
Steering	Burman recirculating ball type steering, 17″ Bluemel adjustable wheel. Left or right-hand steering optional.
Wheels and tyres	Pressed steel bolt-on disc wheels with Dunlop 6.00 x 16″ road speed tyres. Early cars – 5″ wide, later cars $5^{1}/_{2}$″.
Fuel supply	By large delivery S.U. electric pump from a 15 gallon rear tank with petrol level warning light.
Electrical equipment	Lucas de luxe throughout, 12 volt, 64 amp. capacity, twin batteries with constant voltage controlled ventilated dynamo, 10 hour discharge, flush fitting headlamps and wing lamps, stop light, reverse light, twin rear lights, panel light, fitted interior light, twin blended-note horns, twin-blade wiper, cigar lighter, starter motor, vacuum and centrifugal automatic ignition advance.
Instruments	5″ dia 140 mph speedometer, 5″ dia rev counter, ammeter, oil pressure gauge, water temperature gauge, petrol gauge with warning light, electric clock.
Performance	Contemporary figures varied enormously. 0 - 60 12.0 secs 0 - 100 35.3 secs Standing $1/4$ mile – 17.3 secs. Max Speed 120.0 mph 30 - 50 (Top) 7.8 secs Overall fuel consumption 19.8 mpg
Dimensions	Wheelbase 8ft 6in Track 4ft 3in (front) 4ft 2in (rear) Overall length 14ft 5in Width 5ft $1^{1}/_{2}$in Height 4ft $4^{1}/_{2}$in Weight (dry) $26^{1}/_{2}$cwt Ground clearance $7^{1}/_{8}$in
Prices – Basic (new) with Purchase Tax	OTS £998 FHC £1,088 DHC £1,160 OTS £1,263 FHC £1,694 DHC £1,616

XK 140 (where different from XK 120)

Period current	All models 1954-57.		

Chassis Numbers	RHD	LHD	
OTS From	800001	810001	("A" prefix indicates
FHC	804001	814001	S.E. model, "S" – S.E.
DHC	807001	817001	with C-type head)

Numbers Manufactured	OTS	FHC	DHC
RHD	73 (47 U.K. market)	843	479
LHD	3281	1965	2310

Engine
190 bhp at 5,500 rpm.
Special Equipment (with C-type head) 210 bhp at 5,750 rpm.

Transmission
As late XK 120
Optional Overdrive – Overdrive 3.19; top 4.09; 3rd 5.59; 2nd 8.11; 1st and reverse 15.34.

Suspension
Telescopic rear shock absorbers.

Brakes
Friction lining area 189 sq. ins.

Steering
Rack and pinion, rubber mounted on chassis.

Fuel supply
14 gallon fuel tank.

Electrical equipment
Single 12 volt battery (OTS & DHC), integral stop/tail lamps with built-in reflectors, two-speed screen wipers.

Performance
FHC – S.E. model with Overdrive
0 - 60 11.0 secs.   0 - 100 29.5 secs.
Standing $1/4$ mile – 17.4 secs.
Max Speed 129.25 mph   30 - 50 (Top) – 7.4 secs
Overall fuel consumption – 21.7 mpg

Dimensions
Track 4ft $3^1/2''$ (front)   4 ft $2^1/2''$ (rear)
Overall length 14ft 8in   Width 5ft $4^1/2$in
Heights OTS 4ft $5^1/2$in, FHC & DHC 4ft 7in
Weights OTS $24^1/2$ cwts.; FHC $25^1/2$ cwts.; DHC $26^1/2$ cwts.

Prices – Basic (new) with Purchase Tax			
	OTS £1,127,	FHC £1,140,	DHC £1,160
	OTS £1,598,	FHC £1,616,	DHC £1.664

JAGUAR

wins First Alpine Gold Cup ever awarded in Europe's most gruelling Trial

To crown his achievements in a long series of successes, Trials, driver Mr. Ian Appleyard has become the first to gain the Golden Coupe des Alpes, an award of the highest merit for completing three successive Annual Alpine Trials *without the loss of a single mark*. This outstanding feat has been achieved on the same Jaguar XK120 car which has now exceeded a mileage of 45,000 and with which Mr. Appleyard has gained over 40 awards in major International competitions. Measure of its reliability is emphasised by the fact that out of 95 entrants only 23 cars finished this arduous Alpine course, out of which Jaguars gained 1st, 2nd, 3rd and 4th places in their class, and returned fastest times of the day in five out of the six timed tests.

Write for details to Distributors for *States West of Mississippi*: Charles H. Hornburg, Jr., 9176 Sunset Boulevard, Los Angeles, Cal. *Eastern States*: The Hoffman Motor Car Co., Inc., 487 Park Avenue, New York, 22, and at Esquire Building, South Water Street, Chicago.

JAGUAR

XK SUPER SPORTS

ROAD TEST

AUTOMOBILE
ENGINEER

THE JAGUAR XK120

A Super High-speed Car of Exceptional Controllability and Comfort

The Jaguar XK120 two-seater.

IN appraising the design, perform-ance and handling of the Jaguar XK120, it is difficult to realise that the price is only £988. More-over, although the car is described as a "super sports" vehicle, there is no doubt that the term is misleading in that it gives no hint of the true charac-ter of a car in which comfort, smooth-ness, and refinement are associated with an all-round performance sub-stantially in excess of anything offered in a standard production vehicle.

It would be unfortunate if a flaw-less appearance, and the remarkable performance figures, among which may be noted a maximum speed in the neighbourhood of 125 miles an hour and an acceleration time from rest to 100 miles an hour of about 30 seconds, were allowed to obscure other qualities of more practical sig-nificance in everyday use. Of these, the suspension, sweet running, and flexibility would be quite outstanding in cars of much less performance and far higher price. Indeed it is in the suspension and steering that the car offers perhaps the greatest technical interest. Superb handling has been attained not by reason of any radical departure in layout, but on account of the excellent compromise that has been made in the control of a sus-pension relatively soft for the type of car. Accurate and decisive steering

at high speeds is coupled with a light-ness of touch right down to manœuv-ring conditions. The vehicle gives an impressive feeling of complete confi-dence and control that is apparent

SPECIFICATION

ENGINE. Six cylinders. Bore and stroke 83 mm. by 106 mm. Swept volume 3,442 c.c. Maximum b.h.p. 160 at 5,200 r.p.m. Maximum b.m.e.p. and torque 140 lb. per sq. in. and 195 lb. ft. at 2,500 r.p.m. Compression ratio 7 : 1 or 8 : 1. Seven bearing crankshaft. Twin overhead camshafts driven by two-stage duplex roller chain. Twin S.U. carburettors.
CLUTCH. Borg and Beck single dry plate 10in diameter.
GEARBOX. Four speeds and reverse with constant load synchromesh on top, third and second. Ratios : top, 1 : 1 ; third, 1·367 : 1 ; second, 1·982 : 1 ; first and reverse, 3·375 : 1.
REAR AXLE. E.N.V. banjo type with hypoid gears. Alternative ratios 3·27, 3·64, 3·92, 4·3 or 4·56 to 1.
SUSPENSION : Front—wishbones and torsion bars with anti-roll bar. Rear—semi-elliptic springs in conjunction with Hotchkiss drive.
BRAKES. Lockheed hydraulic, two leading shoe at the front. Brake drum diameter and effective width 12in × 2¼in. Friction area 207 sq. in.
TYRES. Dunlop Road Speed 6·00—16. Pressed steel wheels, five stud mounting.
DIMENSIONS. Wheelbase 102in. Track—front 50⅜in at ground, rear 50in. Turning circle 31ft. Ground clearance 7½in. Weight, dry, 2,800 lb.

from the moment of first driving the car.

Without restating the case so often made in the *Automobile Engineer* concerning the contribution to the improvement of the automobile made by the pure racing car in recent years, it may be said that soft suspension, light steering and a pronounced un-dersteer characteristic constitute the general trend in essentially touring car development over the last fifteen years. These characteristics are ad-mirably blended in the Jaguar XK120 and the record of the car in compe-tition, even at this early stage in the life of the design, is evidence of the quality of the vehicle. The behaviour of the car in this respect is not inferior to that of vehicles designed on what may be called the classical sports car principle, in which comfort is sacri-ficed to controllability.

This excellent balance in suspen-sion and steering is a vindication of the logical process of development in which the desirable principles of tour-ing car suspension have been co-ordinated and refined to a point where safe and comfortable travel can be maintained at speeds well beyond any-thing at present conceivable in daily transport.

It is the more surprising therefore that the Jaguar chassis should be so entirely orthodox in conception and

**AUTOMOBILE
ENGINEER**

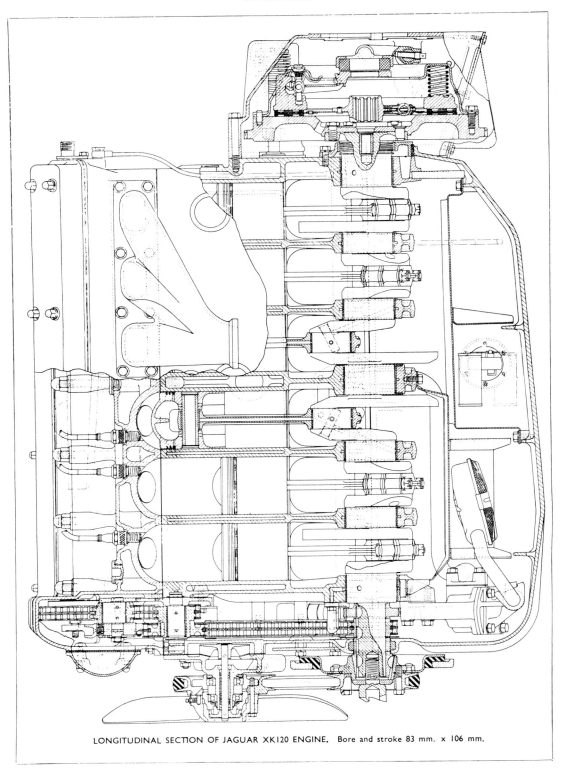

LONGITUDINAL SECTION OF JAGUAR XK120 ENGINE. Bore and stroke 83 mm. x 106 mm.

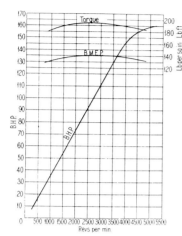

Performance curves.

AUTOMOBILE ENGINEER

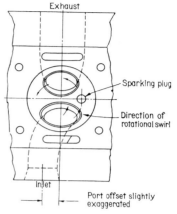

Plan of inlet and exhaust ports.

layout, and upon superficial examination exhibits nothing that would suggest unusual performance. There is, however, much evidence of great care and judgment in detail design, and doubtless it is here that the reasons must be sought for the quite exceptional character of the car. It is in fact so good, that some restraint is necessary in describing its charm. Without indulgence in too many superlatives, however, it must be admitted that the advent of a vehicle of this kind in which *all* the desirable attributes are combined, is something of an event. From nowhere else in the world is such a car forthcoming, and the prestige of British industry is correspondingly raised.

Engine

The six-cylinder engine has a bore and stroke of 83 mm. by 106 mm. (3·27in by 4·17in), giving a swept volume of 3442 c.c. (210 cu in) and a piston area of 50·4 sq in. A compression ratio of either 7 to 1 or 8 to 1 is employed and with the 8 to 1 ratio the maximum b.h.p. is 160 at 5,200 r.p.m. while the maximum b.m.e.p. and torque is 140 lb per sq in and 195 lb ft at 2,500 r.p.m. The dry weight of engine and gearbox is 640 lb, of which the gearbox accounts for 110 lb.

Made in chrome cast iron, the cylinder block and crankcase forms an integral unit ex-

tending down to the crankshaft centre-line, the seven main bearing housings being not only well ribbed vertically, but also tied to the crankcase wall by fillets of generous radius, as shown in the illustration. There are full length water jackets with a separate gallery along the near-side, into which the water pump delivers directly. Water spaces are provided between adjacent bores. The cylinder bores are machined with a single point tool and finished by honing.

Each main bearing cap is secured by two $\frac{1}{2}$in diameter bolts and located by two dowels. A circumferential oil groove in the caps and housings s provided for distribution of the feed behind the bearing shells, which are of Vandervell steel-backed white metal type, having single circumferential oil grooves with two feed holes in each half bearing. The main oil gallery and cross feeds to the main bearings are formed by drillings in the casting.

Of En.16 manganese molybdenum steel, the crankshaft, which is, of course, statically and dynamically balanced, has journal diameters of 2·75in and crankpin diameters of 2·088in. The effective crankpin length is 0·97in, while the journals have the following effective lengths: front, centre and rear 1·5in, intermediate 1in. Crankshaft end thrust is taken by steel-backed white metal strips carried on each face of the centre bearing.

Behind the rear main bearing is an oil flinger and return thread, the crankshaft terminating in a flange to which the flywheel is attached. The clutch spigot bearing is of porous bronze. A separate split housing surrounds the return thread, the upper part being secured to the rear face of the cylinder block, while the lower part, located by two dowels, forms a joint with the sump.

Beyond the front main bearing the crankshaft carries the oil pump and distributor drive skew gear, the camshaft drive sprocket, an oil thrower, a

sealing collar, and a taper sleeve on which is mounted the Metalastik bonded rubber, torsional vibration damper to which the fan pulley is also attached. These individual components at the front of the crankshaft are located by single Woodruff keys with the exception of the damper mounting cone, which has two Woodruff keys. The whole assembly is pulled up against the front journal by means of a washer behind the starting handle dog and the oil seal is formed by graphited asbestos housed in the crankcase and sump.

Diagonal drillings from the journals lead to $\frac{29}{64}$in diameter blind bores in the crankpins. The feed to the big-ends is by means of a transverse hole drilled right across the pin so that in effect there are two feed holes. Since these holes are well inside the maximum radius described by the crankpin bores, an effective sludge trap is provided that would be unlikely to interfere with the oil flow to the bearing.

Made in En.16 the connecting rods have a centre distance of 7·75in and the single ribbed caps are located by fitted bolts. Oil is fed to the small end through a $\frac{3}{16}$in diameter drilling. As in the case of the main bearings, the big-end bearings are of Vandervell steel-backed white metal type.

The Aerolite aluminium alloy solid skirt pistons are tin-plated and each carry two compression rings

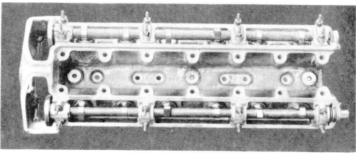

Cylinder head with camshafts in position.

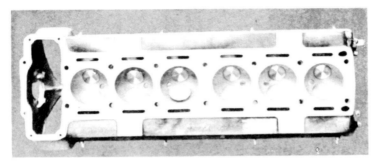

Cylinder head showing combustion chambers.

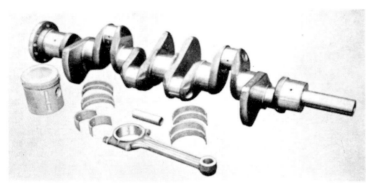

Piston, connecting rod, crankshaft and bearings.

Cylinder block and crankcase showing main bearing housings.

and one slotted scraper ring, the upper ring being chromium plated. Fully floating gudgeon pins made in case-hardened steel are $\frac{7}{8}$in. in diameter and are located by internal circlips.

Secured to the cylinder block by fourteen $\frac{3}{8}$in diameter waisted studs, the cylinder head is of aluminium alloy in RR.50. In addition to the main studs there are six smaller studs securing the front end of the head. The combustion chambers are approximately hemispherical and the general design of the valve ports, induction system and combustion chambers has been carried out in collaboration with Weslake & Co., Ltd.

The accompanying illustration shows the port layout in which the off-set of the inlet port has been slightly exaggerated. Control of turbulence is brought about by the curved sides of the inlet port and the degree of swirl can be controlled by an increase or decrease in the rate of curvature of these walls.

It will be seen that the port entry is tapered to increase the velocity of the charge from the induction pipe and to produce a piled effect by making use of the kinetic energy of the charge. This first zone is followed by a second zone around the valve guide shaped to decrease the obstruction caused by the guide. The third zone is the inlet valve seat which has a radiused entry to the valve seat proper. This, in conjunction with the valve shape, gives the highest possible flow at low valve lift.

It is claimed that the control of turbulence provided in this engine permits the burning of lean mixtures and over the normal speed range of the engine at 75 per cent full load the fuel consumption need not exceed 0·47 pints per b.h.p. hour and at 50 per cent load, 0·52 pints per b.h.p. hour. Under full load conditions the maximum power fuel consumption is between 0·5 and 0·53 pints per b.h.p. hour and an economy setting giving 0·47 pints per b.h.p. hour can be used with some loss in brake mean effective pressure.

The valves are set at an included angle of 70 deg and are operated from twin overhead camshafts by cylindrical tappets made in chill cast iron, with tappet bearings also of cast iron and a shrink fit in the cylinder head. The valves seat on Brimol inserts shrunk in by heating the head in oil. The seat angles are 30 deg for the inlet and 45 deg for the exhaust. The inlet valves are of En.52 silicon chrome steel and have a throat diameter of $1\frac{3}{8}$in and a lift of $\frac{5}{16}$in, whereas the exhaust valves are in Fox 1282 austenitic steel and have a throat diameter of $1\frac{1}{4}$in and a lift of $\frac{5}{16}$in.

AUTOMOBILE
ENGINEER

Valve timing is as follows:

Inlet opens 15 deg before top dead centre.

Inlet closes 57 deg after bottom dead centre.

Exhaust opens 57 deg before bottom dead centre.

Exhaust closes 15 deg after top dead centre.

The firing order is 1, 5, 3, 6, 2, 4, No. 1 cylinder being at the rear.

Both valve guides project slightly into the ports, the exhaust guide having an enlarged bore for a depth of about $\frac{1}{16}$in at the inner end. Duplex valve springs retained by split collars are employed, and the valve clearance is set by means of adjusting pads between the tappets and valve stems. When cold the valve clearances are 0·006in for the inlet and 0·008in for the exhaust.

Made in chill cast iron, the two camshafts are each carried in four bearings having Vandervell steel-backed white metal liners. From the crankshaft, double roller chains of 0·375in pitch with $\frac{1}{4}$in rollers provide a two-stage drive for the camshafts. The first stage has a blade-type tensioner and drives an intermediate sprocket keyed to the hub of the second stage driving sprocket.

The second stage chain passes around the two camshaft sprockets, in between which is placed an idler sprocket mounted on an eccentric spindle whereby the chain tension can be adjusted. Access to the idler adjustment is gained by removing the breather housing on the front face of the cylinder head, adjustment being effected by slackening a locknut on the idler spindle and rotating a serrated plate. Two spring-loaded plungers carried in the spindle support bracket provide location for the serrated plate in steps equivalent to half the pitch of the serrations. The plate is, of course, so mounted on the spindle that rotation of the plate rotates the spindle. Both the idler sprocket and the second stage drive sprocket have steel-backed white metal bushes in the bores.

The camshaft sprockets are each attached to flanges on the ends of the camshafts by means of two setscrews. Each sprocket consists of a rim on which the teeth are formed, and a hub

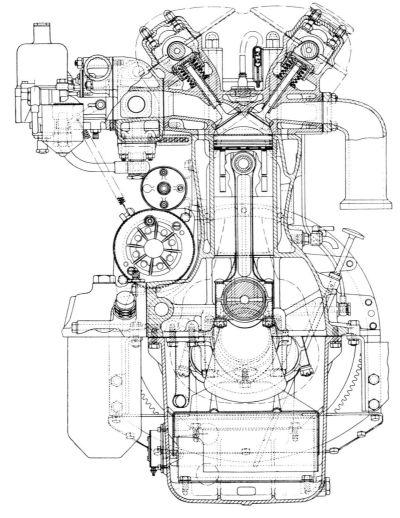

Cross section of XK120 engine. Bore and stroke 83 mm. x 106 mm.

**AUTOMOBILE
ENGINEER**

Near-side of XK120 power unit.

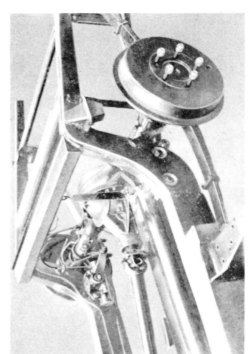

Rear axle and suspension.

Off-side of XK120 power unit.

Independent front suspension assembly.

AUTOMOBILE ENGINEER

built up from the two discs forming an adjuster plate having a central guide pin that projects through a slot in the idler support bracket and terminating in a threaded end. The sprocket rim spigots on to the camshaft flange and has internal serrations in the bore of its own shallow flange. These engage serrations on the periphery of one of the discs forming the adjuster plate, while the second disc, of larger diameter, rests against the front face of the rim flange and is retained there by means of an internal circlip. The two setscrews, by means of which the sprocket assembly is secured to the camshaft flange, pass through clearance holes in the adjuster plate.

To set the valve timing, No. 1 piston is brought to top dead centre on the firing stroke and the camshafts are turned until keyways formed in their flanges behind the front bearings engage with tongues in setting gauges. The sprockets, with chain in position, are placed on the camshafts and the adjuster plates are withdrawn until the serrations disengage. The plates are then rotated until their holes for the set pins coincide with the tapped holes in the camshaft flanges. After re-engaging the serrations and installing the circlips the set pins are inserted and locked with wire.

It should be noted that removal and replacement of the cylinder head is carried out without disturbing the valve timing. It is only necessary to slacken the chain adjuster, remove the set pins from the sprockets, withdraw the sprockets from the camshafts and slide them along the slots in the brackets. After placing clamping nuts on the guide pins to hold them in the slots, the head can be removed. The adjustment of chain tension and valve timing will be evident from study of the illustrations.

Driven from a skew gear at the front end of the camshaft is the distributor and oil pump drive shaft. The gear-type oil pump draws oil from the DTD.424 die cast sump through a floating inlet and delivers through a separate pipe to the Tecalemit full flow filter where the relief valve is also accessibly placed. From here the oil enters the main gallery drilled along the offside of the crank-

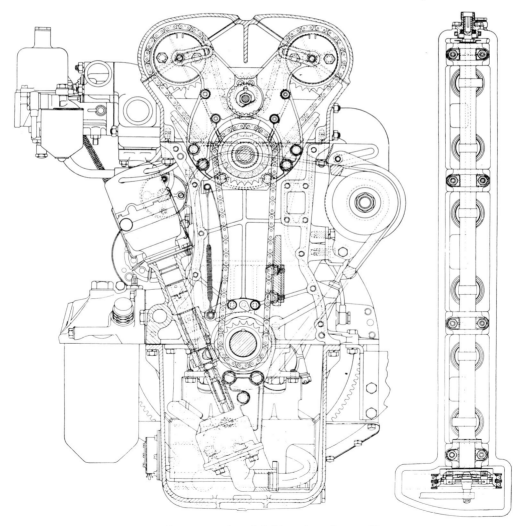

Arrangement of camshaft drive and sprocket assembly.

AUTOMOBILE ENGINEER

Off-side view of XK120 chassis.

case and is fed through transverse drillings to annular grooves in the main bearing housings and caps, from which it feeds into the bearings through four holes in the bearing shells. Thence the oil passes through the crankshaft drillings to the connecting rod big-ends and so to the small ends via the drillings in the connecting rod shanks. A continuation of the cross drilling to the rear main bearing feeds an external pipe on the near-side of the engine by means of which oil is led to the rear camshaft bearings. From here it feeds into longitudinal drillings in the camshafts, from which appropriate cross drillings in the journals provide a feed to each camshaft bearing.

The cams dip into the overflow from the bearings and the oil returns to the crankcase from the front end of the head, flooding the upper camshaft drive chain. The intermediate and idler sprocket spindles are drilled longitudinally and transversely to provide an oil feed to the sprocket bushes. Oil returning from the cylinder head is collected in troughs formed in the idler brackets and feeding the spindle drillings via drillings in the bracket. Lubrication of the first stage chain is provided by jets fed from a drilling leading off the oil supply to the front main bearing. A jet is also provided here for the oil pump and distributor drive skew gears. The sump capacity is 24 pints.

Cooling system

Water from the pump is delivered to a gallery running along the nearside of the cylinder block from which passages into the head direct water around the faces of the combustion chambers and across to the off-side of the head past the sparking plug bosses. The water emerges through four holes along the off-side face of the head into the induction manifold jackets, from which it finally returns to the header tank. It will be evident that the forced circulation is confined to the cylinder head and induction manifold, while the water surrounding the cylinder bores remains relatively undisturbed.

The induction manifold has a full

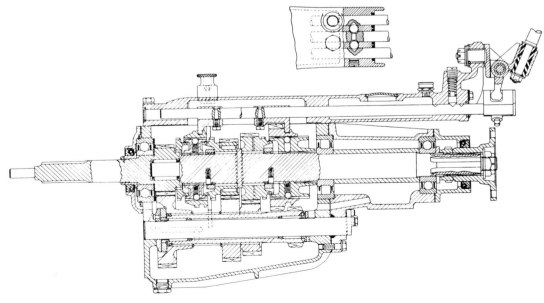

Arrangement of gear box.

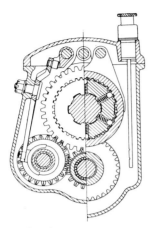

Gear box cross section.

length water jacket along its top face and there is a shorter jacket along the bottom face under Nos. 3 and 4 ports. There are also water pockets formed between Nos. 1 and 2 and 5 and 6 ports on the inner side face of the manifold.

The water pump spindle driven by the fan pulley, which is carried on two ball bearings, has a synthetic rubber seal. At the rear end separate greasers are provided for the ball bearing and spindle. A by-pass thermostat is embodied in the system.

Ignition

Ignition is by Lucas coil and distributor and Champion type NA8 14mm sparking plugs set with gaps

of 0·022in. The distributor has centrifugal and vacuum advance and the timing is set at 5 deg before top dead centre fully retarded, with the vernier adjustment in the midway position. An advance range of 11 to 13 deg on the distributor is provided by the vacuum system while the centrifugal advance mechanism has the following characteristics:—On engines of 7 to 1 compression ratio the advance range on the distributor is 16 to 18 deg with full advance at 1,400 r.p.m. On 8 to 1 compression ratio engines the advance range is 13 to 15 deg on the distributor with full advance at 1,600 r.p.m.

An S.U. electric petrol pump supplies the twin horizontal S.U. carburettors, which have a bore of 1¾in. There is also an auxiliary starting carburettor with automatic thermo-electric operation.

The aluminium alloy induction manifold is of the six-port type with the induction tract of rectangular section. Midway along the tract is a balance restriction having a circular hole, and at this point the mixture from the starting carburettor is delivered.

Clutch

Enclosed in a DTD.424 aluminium alloy bell housing, the clutch is a single plate Borg and Beck unit with 10in diameter disc and conventional carbon block type of withdrawal bearing.

Gearbox

The gearbox provides four forward speeds and reverse and has constant-load type of synchromesh mechanism on top, third and second speeds. It is of conventional design and is operated by a remote control lever. The gear ratios are as follows:—top 1:1, third 1·367:1, second 1·982:1, first 3·375:1.

Carried in a cast iron main casing, the shafts are at 3¼in centre distance.

Rear anchorage of torsion bar.

A light alloy casting encloses the rear end of the mainshaft which extends for a distance of about 8in behind the roller bearing in the gearbox main casing. Its outer end is supported by a ball bearing in the extension casing, while the spigot bearing in the first motion shaft bore is of the needle roller type. Needle rollers are also employed to support the third and second speed mainshaft gears. Both the first motion shaft and constant pinion and the mainshaft are in Fox 040 Hicore 90 steel, as is the layshaft with which is formed the first speed pinion. All other gears are also in Fox 040.

The dog rings and operating sleeves are in Fox 031 Hicore 75 and it is of interest to note that the synchromesh sleeves in En.36 have no bronze facings. The cone included angle is 10 deg. and the oil grooves on the dog rings consist of thirty-six axial grooves 0·04in wide and 0·02in deep, and a right-hand thread of 0·02in pitch,

Arrangement of hypoid bevel rear axle.

AUTOMOBILE
ENGINEER

Rear view of front suspension.

0·009in deep, 0·01in wide at the top and having an included angle of 42 deg. The gears have a diametral pitch of 10 circular, equivalent to a normal D.P. of 10·86, a 20 deg. pressure angle, and the constant mesh third and second speed gears all have a right-hand helix angle of 23 deg. The face widths are as follows:—constant mesh and third speed gears 1in, second speed gears 31/32in, first speed gear $\frac{13}{16}$in. Needle roller bearings support the layshaft assembly with end location by means of chill cast phosphor bronze thrust washers butting against thrust pads of En.36T normalized. There are no unusual features in the selector mechanism, which has die-cast aluminium bronze forks and interlocking of the selector rods by means of two balls and a plunger, as shown in the arrangement drawing.

Rear axle

Alternative ratios are available in the E.N.V. hypoid bevel rear axle, namely 3·27, 3·64, 3·92, 4·3 or 4·56 to 1. The axle is of the banjo type with semi-floating shafts made in En.19 and tapering from 1in diameter behind the splines to 1$\frac{1}{8}$in diameter at the inner oil seal. The outer ends of the shafts are up-set to form the brake drum and wheel mounting flanges which carry five $\frac{1}{2}$in diameter wheel studs. Both the main gear casing and the differential cage are made in Lepaz malleable iron, while crown wheel and pinion are made in En.34 and En.35A respectively. The two-pinion differential has En.33 pinions and gears, while the spider is in 3S 15. The inner ends of the axle shafts butt against a thrust block and the taper roller hub bearings are shimmed between the bearing housing and brake back plate to give 0·002-0·004in axle shaft end play. Adjustment of the differential taper roller bearings is by means of ring

nuts, while the pinion shaft, which is also carried in taper roller bearings, is provided with shims behind the outer race of the inner bearings.

Suspension

Before treating the front and rear suspensions individually, it may be of interest to consider the suspension as a whole and its influence on the handling characteristics of the car. Table I shows the relative characteristics, and it will be seen that the front suspension is somewhat softer than the rear.

The front/rear weight proportion is 45·5/54·5 per cent, based on a loading of driver and passenger, oil and water but no petrol.

The general layout is designed to result in a condition of under-steer and to this end the anti-roll bar is fitted on the front suspension and the rear springs are inclined downwards towards the front at an angle of 7$\frac{3}{4}$ deg. At the front the roll centre is within $\frac{1}{2}$in of ground level, while the height of the rear roll centre is about 9$\frac{3}{4}$in. The height of the centre of gravity of the sprung mass is about 18in, giving a moment arm about the roll axis of 13in. The height of the centre of gravity of the unsprung masses, that is to say, the front wheels and suspension linkage, and also the rear axle, is 13$\frac{1}{2}$in.

The roll stiffness of the front suspension is 6,050 lb in per deg, and of the rear suspension 1,730 lb in per deg, giving a total roll stiffness of 7,780 lb in per deg. Taking a lateral acceleration of 1·0 g for convenience, the resultant roll angle is 5·1 deg, and the total roll transfer on the front tyres is 606·5 lb, made up of 561 lb due to the sprung mass and 45·5 lb due to the unsprung mass. The total roll transfer on the rear tyres is 529·5 lb, made up of 162·5 lb due to the

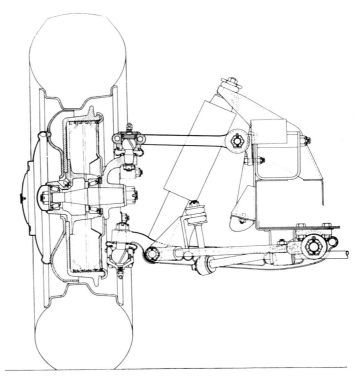

Elevation of front suspension.

AUTOMOBILE ENGINEER

AUTOMOBILE ENGINEER

TABLE I

	Front	Rear
Total weight per wheel ..	710 lb.	845 lb.
Unsprung weight per wheel	110 lb.	155 lb.
Sprung weight per wheel ..	600 lb.	690 lb.
Effective static deflection ..	5½in.	5in.
Nominal frequency* ..	80 oscillations per minute.	84 oscillations per minute.
Static stress in spring ..	56,500 lb. per sq. in.	88,000 lb. per sq. in.

* These figures take into account the effect of the rubber bushes in the suspension linkages.

Front suspension and track rod layout.

moment of the sprung mass about the roll axis, 270 lb due to the side thrust of the sprung mass operating at the rear roll centre, 84 lb due to the rear unsprung weight and 13 lb due to the front unsprung weight.

It is of interest to note the contribution made by the anti-roll bar. Thus the front suspension rate in rolling is 265 lb per in, while the rear suspension rate in rolling is 138 lb per in. The stabilizer rate is 150 lb per in and the force transfer due to the stabilizer amounts to 345 lb out of the total front transfer of 605·5 lb.

In normal circumstances the high proportion of the overturning couple carried by the front tyres should en-sure that the self-aligning torque is adequate without the assistance of any appreciable castor angle. However, to meet conditions of sustained high speeds, it is necessary for satisfactory tyre life to increase the normal tyre pressures of 25 lb per sq in to 35 lb per sq in. This substantially reduces the self-aligning torque and in fact a castor angle of 3 deg is pro-vided. This might be expected to result in rather heavy steering when normal tyre pressures are employed, but in practice the effect is not noticeable. Doubtless the reason may be found in the high efficiency of the Burman re-circulating ball type of steering gear, and also in the design of the stub axle swivel joints, which are spherical joints having a spread of about 8⅞in and probably result in appreciably less friction compared with more conventional designs.

Front suspension

Torsion bars in conjunction with wishbones form the basis of the independent front suspension, which has a total movement of 7in made up of 3½in bump and 3½in rebound. Damping is provided by Newton direct acting dampers and the inner wishbone pivot points each have opposed Metalastik BC type conical bonded rubber bushes. Each wishbone is made up of two separate arms, the upper assembly having an effective length of 8¾in with a spread at the inner end of 7¾in. The two separate wishbone arms in En.8Q are bolted together at their outer extremities with the upper ball housing interposed. The lower wishbone assembly comprises a rear member of I-section in En.16T to which is bolted the internally splined torsion bar flange. The lower front wishbone lever or stay rod in mild steel is of circular section ⅝in diameter and is bolted to the rear member at a point adjacent to the outer end. The spread of the inner lower wishbone

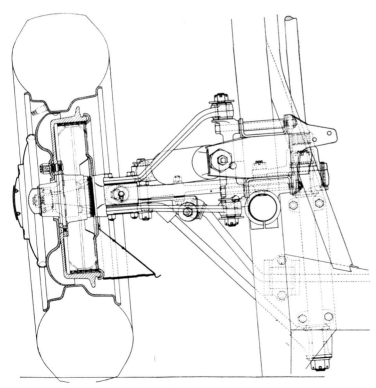

Plan of front suspension.

Three-quarter rear view of chassis.

bearings is 13in and the effective length is 15in.

The screwed pin connecting the lower wishbone levers at their outer ends is extended rearwards to form the attachment point for the lower end of the damper, where there is a rubber bush, while a bracket carrying the connecting link to the anti-roll bar is also partly located off the same pin. The lower wishbone terminates in a taper seating for the lower ball pin which, as in the case of the upper pin, is made in En.24T. The lower ball pin, which is hard chrome plated, seats on spherical seatings made in Ferrobestos LA3, an asbestos and plastic material impregnated with graphite. Whereas the upper ball housing embodies spring loading of

the spherical seating, the lower ball socket has a cap attached to the stub axle carrier by means of four set-screws and located by a spigot ring with shims interposed between the socket cap and stub axle carrier. The En.16T stub axle shaft is located in the En.16T stub axle carrier by means of a taper and locknut and carries the Timken taper roller hub bearings. The hub itself is in Ley's blackheart malleable iron. A castor angle of 3 deg is provided, with adjustment by means of shims interposed between the upper wishbone arms and the ball housing. Camber is also adjustable by means of shims interposed between the upper wishbone shaft and the frame bracket, the normal setting being $1\frac{3}{4}$ to 2 deg. The effective

swivel centreline inclination is 5 deg.

Made in En.45 silico manganese steel ground bar by the English Steel Corporation, the torsion bars have a working length of 47·25in and a diameter of 0·930in. They are shot peened, pre-stressed in the direction of twist and finished with a coat of protective "flexible" paint. The ends of the bars are splined and locate at the front end in flanges bolted to the rear lower wishbone members. At their rear ends the torsion bars locate in the splined bores of reaction levers, the forked ends of which bear on thrust pads and adjusting nuts carried by long bolts, the heads of which seat in the centre cross member. Clockwise rotation of the adjusting nuts increases the ground clearance and *vice*

Three-quarter front view of chassis.

AUTOMOBILE
ENGINEER

Hand brake lever and petrol pump mounting.

versa. The reaction levers each carry a locking set-bolt working in a slot in the cross member. Should the correct setting be unobtainable within the limits of movement permitted by the slot, the torsion bar can be repositioned in relation to the rear wishbone mounting flange. When correctly set, a clearance of $7\frac{1}{8}$in is provided under the lower face of the frame side member at a point just behind the engine sump.

Carried in a trunnion on the upper wishbone bracket is the Burman re-circulating ball steering gear, the steering column being very well raked at an angle of only 10 deg to the horizontal. The drop arm projects forwards and is linked to a corresponding slave drop arm on the opposite side of the car by the centre member of the three-piece track rod, as shown in the illus-

tration, the slave drop arm spindle being carried in a long plain bush located by a screw-thread. Silentbloc bearings are used at the ends of the drop arms where the centre track rod member is attached. A toe-in of $\frac{1}{8}$in to $\frac{3}{16}$in is the normal setting. For all practical purposes the track rod end sections describe true arcs, and no roll steer effects are embodied.

Rear suspension

Having five leaves 7/32in thick and two leaves $\frac{3}{16}$in thick, the rear springs are made in En.45 silico manganese steel and have speared and tapered tips. There are no interleaves, but gaiters are fitted. The spring eyes have rubber bushes, as also have the shackle bearings.

The springs are sloped downwards towards the front at an angle of $7\frac{3}{4}$ deg to introduce an under-steer effect from the resultant skewing of the axle in rolling conditions and the axle is also offset towards the front of the spring, so that the spring measures 20in from the axle to the front anchorage and 24in to the shackle attachment. The reason for this is to impart a necessary downward tilt of the axle nose-piece to maintain constant angles between the propeller shaft joints. Girling lever type dampers are operated by short links on brackets on the axle casing. Bump rubbers and check straps limit the axle movement to $3\frac{1}{2}$in bump and $3\frac{1}{2}$in rebound from the normal position.

Frame

The frame is of conventional design with deep box-section side members having a maximum depth of $6\frac{1}{2}$in and

Rear spring anchorage.

a width of $3\frac{1}{2}$in. Two very substantial box-section cross members are provided, one at the front and one at the centre, while at the rear end of the frame a somewhat lighter member spans the frame at the top of the up-sweep and a tubular member behind the petrol tank extends beyond the side members and carries the attachment points for the rear spring shackles.

At the front end the inner closing plates are swept in to meet the rear face of the front cross member at points about $7\frac{1}{2}$in apart. Just beyond the point where the insweep begins are welded the brackets carrying the upper wishbone and engine mounting supports and also the anchorage points for the dampers. Aft of the centre cross member the rear portions of the side members are set parallel. The outer members of the box sec-

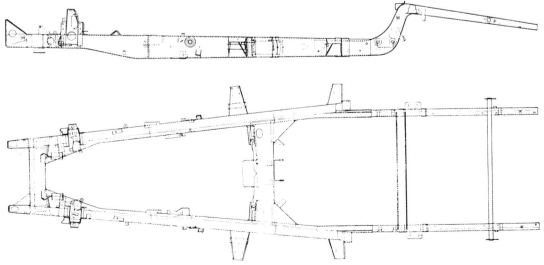

Layout of XK120 frame.

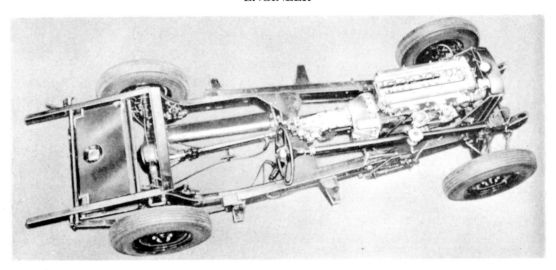

AUTOMOBILE
ENGINEER

Semi-plan view of chassis.

tion, however, are continued for a short distance on their diverging line to provide a very substantial anchorage for the rear springs in the form of an open-ended box giving unusually good support for the spring eye through-bolts.

Brakes

Lockheed hydraulic brakes are fitted, those at the front being of the two leading shoe type and giving a front to rear braking proportion of 60/40. The 12in diameter brake drums are of copper iron and the Mintex M.15 brake linings are $11\frac{1}{2}$in long by $2\frac{1}{4}$in wide, giving a total area of 207 sq in. In a car of this type braking presents a particularly difficult problem and it will be noted that air scoops are fitted to the back plates of the front brake drums to assist cooling. There are corresponding slots in the bodywork to ensure maximum effect.

A fly-off type of handbrake lever is provided, operating the rear wheel brakes by means of a cable.

Dimensions

Wheelbase, 102in; track—front $50\frac{5}{8}$ in at ground, rear 50in; turning circle, 31ft; ground clearance, $7\frac{1}{8}$in; dry weight, 2,800 lb.

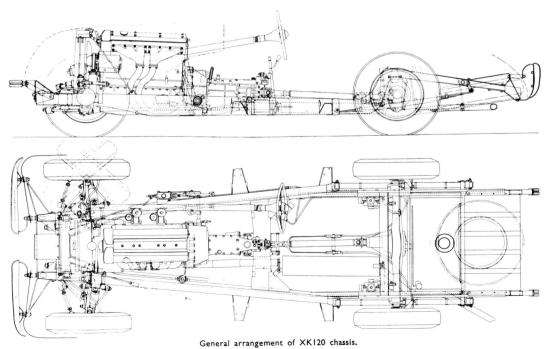

General arrangement of XK120 chassis.

The XK 120 interior with its leather seats and covered dashboard complete with full carpeting and a comprehensive selection of instruments was considered lavish for a roadster in the late forties.

This shot of the inside of a Roadster door shows the method of fixing the sidescreen, which had a small flap below the transparent section to allow hand signals.

These simple, classic lines conceal a great deal of work in restoration, but the result is unquestionably worthwhile. The front wings are beautiful pieces of art but difficult to reproduce with their myriad compound curves.

The dramatic rise and fall of the 120s wing line can clearly be seen and although the hood did nothing to improve the overall shape, it at least gave some protection from the elements.

Early engines did not have studs around the front of cam covers and consequently suffered from oil leaks which explains the later non-standard modification on the front of this engine.

The grille was made up of individual rolled folded slats brazed to the surround. Above was mounted the bronze and enamel badge on the bonnet, an item that was always made of aluminium.

The tonneau cover provided some alternative protection from the elements and could, in the usual fashion, be unzipped down the middle.

The word classic is often devalued by over-use these days, but surely the superb shape of the XK 120 meets the precise definition of the word.

The subtle bumpers, delicate sidelights and simple, light grille all contribute to the enduring beauty of Sir William Lyons' masterpiece of the early post-war period.

Far top left:- One of the most successful XKs in competition, and one of the most successful rally cars of all time, was Ian Appleyard's 120 registered, NUB 120.

Above left:- As can be seen the 140 bonnet badge was incorporated in the new grille which, being a cast item was heavier and contained less slats than its predecessor.

Opposite left:- This close up of the boot badge shows that by the time of the 140's introduction, Jaguar were able to boast of two famous Le Mans wins to add to the sundry other XK engined achievements around the globe.

Far bottom left:- The XK 140, seen here in Drophead Coupe form, was evolved from the 120 rather than again being a radical step forward. It was more of a Grand Touring car with both more power and more refinement.

Below:- The rear wing spats are not to everybody's taste these days and many owners, unless competing in a Concours d'Elegance competition, leave them off.

The Drophead and Fixed Head Coupe models were most comfortably appointed with a plush interior more redolent of the pre-war era.

The wide doors give good access and one can see that the protruding horn push of the 120s has been superseded by this rather flatter item fitted to the 140s.

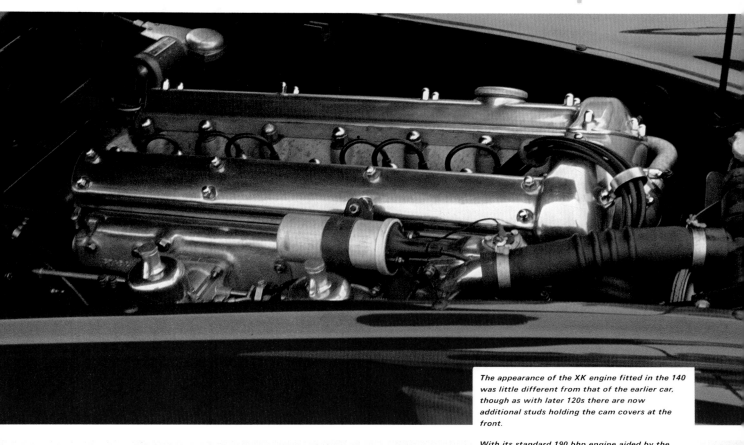

The appearance of the XK engine fitted in the 140 was little different from that of the earlier car, though as with later 120s there are now additional studs holding the cam covers at the front.

With its standard 190 bhp engine aided by the optional overdrive, the XK 140 will very happily consume the ground before it at a genuine 120 mph plus.

457 SPB

The starting point? It may seem frightening but in many ways it is the best course, and at least virtually all parts are now available.

An XK may be a difficult and expensive car to restore, but in viewing and, above all, driving a good XK, one is amply rewarded.

457 SPB

OWNER'S VIEW

Mike Barker has been involved with fast bikes and cars all his life and today he runs the Midland Motor Museum at Bridgnorth in Shropshire. Whilst at college he designed and built his own sports racing car entitled the Alton, which was at first Alta engined and then very successfully Jaguar engined. He has raced a C-type, D-type, DB3S, GT40 and many others. Apart from his XK 120 Roadster, he owns a BMW 328, an E-type, a DBS Vantage and a Lister version of the XJS.

In the late fifties Mike acquired a 1956 XK 140, registration number WAE 586. He remembers he did 35,000 miles in that car at an average of 18.7 m.p.g. and he fondly recalls covering the entire length of the M1, as it was when it first opened, in 35 minutes at an average of 114 m.p.h. In the early seventies he started to search for and found his ex-rally 120, PPE 101.

P.H.P. With all your experience of exotic cars, why do you like the 120?

M.B. It's an interesting car to drive. I enjoy driving it and as a fun car I drive it more than anything else these days. It doesn't hold the road like a modern car and it certainly doesn't stop like a modern car, but so what, it's an early fifties motor car and you can still have a lot of fun with it.

P.H.P. You are in the, perhaps, unique position of owning a 120 and a BMW 328. Certainly Jaguar were playing around with a 328 in the late forties and it has often been cited as an inspiration for the XK. What are your views?

M.B. I'm sure the shape is the main thing that influenced Jaguar because really a 120 is a 328 but longer and lower. The 328 was the first sports car to have an all-enveloping body. I'm not so sure about the mechanical design. The engine was nothing like the BMW one and everyone was using a live rear axle in the late forties. There were minor details they shared, but I would say that it was the shape that they picked up more than anything.

P.H.P. What sort of condition was your 120 in when you bought it?

M.B. I looked at a lot of 120s. Most of them were terrible, but this one had obviously been looked after reasonably well. I took it on knowing it needed a total rebuild, but basically it looked fairly good. I didn't do it all myself but took it to a garage in Surrey that I knew well and they took the body off and started by doing the chassis. That was not too bad, but we worked right through it and didn't do anything to the engine at that stage. The body was not too good and so there was quite a lot of work done on the body. It was retrimmed and I started to run it around and then I found that the engine did need some work doing on it and so completely rebuilt the engine as well. So now we have a 120 that is in pretty reasonable order.

P.H.P. What about spares? Have you had any problems obtaining anything?

M.B. No. The only problem we had when we were rebuilding it was the windscreen pillars. The ones on the car were pretty terrible and we had to search around to find some reasonable ones.

P.H.P. Is there a specialist you have found particularly useful?

M.B. Yes, Aubrey Finburgh (Classic Autos) is always very helpful indeed.

P.H.P. How often do you use the car?

M.B. Never in the winter and about once a fortnight, say, in the summer. I've done some driving tests in it, in fact, Gina and I came 1st and 2nd at the International Jaguar Week a couple of years ago. I've raced it on odd occasions and did the Coronation Rally. I think it is a great shame there are not more XKs raced.

P.H.P. Are you a member of a Jaguar club and do you think it is useful?

M.B. I've been a member of the J.D.C. since the mid-fifties. I enjoy all motor clubs, they are all slightly different. Pretty well every motor club has its ups and downs. I think the grass roots of the Club are the Areas (Area Meetings) and providing they keep going that is the main thing. You have the Registers to look after the owners of individual cars.

P.H.P. What advice would you give to prospective owners?

M.B. I would first get to know someone who has one and is knowledgeable about the car. Make friends with them because to go it alone, unless you are very knowledgable, would be courting disaster.

P.H.P. Finally, Mike, you have owned both a 120 and a 140, which do you prefer?

M.B. I prefer the 120 because it was the first of the line. The 140 was a little more plush, but certainly if I had to hurry a car down a country lane it would be the 120.

John Bridcutt owns an XK 140 Fixed Head and is the enthusiastic and hard-working Secretary of the XK Register. The XK is his only car.

P.H.P. What do you like about XKs?

J.B. Well, I think the character of the car mainly. I was brought up very much on vintage cars in the days gone by, and the concept of a big engine in a chassis working easily with high gearing is to me very attractive. It is a magnificent engine and the body is very beautiful, a wonderful motor car at 75/80 mph, so very relaxed. I love it for that reason, I think, as much as any other.

P.H.P. Why did you choose a 140?

J.B. It is a purely personal thing. I think the 120 is a very pretty car, but the 140 had rack and pinion steering and a little more room inside. The 150 which had disc brakes which were obviously a major step forward, is, in my opinion, not such an attractive car. The 140 was the one in the middle that I really wanted. I also think the XK range is very well made. I have a Fixed Head because being my only car I have to use it in the winter and it's more civilised. The Fixed Heads are so nicely finished inside, even by today's standards and the performance is adequate in today's conditions still. In its own day it was, of course, tremendous. Today you would call it adequate.

P.H.P. What condition was it in when you bought it?

J.B. It had been stored for ten years. It was quite good mechanically as it had only done seventy odd thousand miles with, I think, three owners. I got it back on the road after having done the brakes, having had the head off and fitted a new exhaust system, and it really went very well. We had a little bit of drama with the crankshaft rear cork seal (a common problem). Oil was pouring out of the back, so I took the engine out and found the cork seal was not only badly fitted, but it had gone back 180 degrees on itself so half the radius between the sump and the bearing cap was just not sealed at all. No wonder the oil came out! Having done that it was mechanically pretty good, but bodily it wasn't in good condition. So I got a set of Bill Lawrence panels and had those fitted last year.

It is not a concours car but I think it is quite smart and I can take it out in the winter. I always enjoy taking it out. It seems to go through tyres at an alarming rate. I never seem to get more than about 10,000 miles out of a set.

P.H.P. Any particular problems you have had with the car?

J.B. Oval brake drums! I'd had the drums skimmed out by somebody who was supposed to know what they were doing, but they obviously hadn't done it properly. I had them done again by an engineering firm and you couldn't believe it was the same car. A new set of Konis also worked wonders. The car's now done about 85,000 miles and uses very little oil. I think all the performance is still there and driving at between 75 and 85 mph on a long run it will give me 24 mpg, which is quite incredible I think.

P.H.P. Any particular suppliers you would recommend?

J.B. Well, I mentioned Bill Lawrence just now and I think he is first-class. He was on time and the panels were of good quality. Trevor Scott-Worthington (Coventry Auto Components) is effective and efficient, and has the bits that people want. Bob Smith at R.S. Panels produced a superb set of rear wings, very reasonably priced and, as far as I can see, indistinguishable from the originals.

Bob Davis of Marina Garage does not as yet own an XK, though he hopes to, but he has restored several including Barry Williams' XK 140 Drophead featured in these pages.

P.H.P. What sort of condition was Barry's car in when you first saw it?

R.D. It was drivable and everything was on it. It just looked as though it needed a respray. But once we got the paint off and the body off we could see there were holes everywhere – it was like a colander! People do not believe how bad XKs are until you have got the paint off the car.

P.H.P. What did you have to replace?

R.D. The bonnet, bootlid and bulkhead is all that's left. The rest was replaced or rebuilt. Time is always the biggest problem. Double the time you think it is going to take and you might get somewhere near it. The bodywork takes an incredible time because it's so exacting. It's a very complex body with a lot of lead in it.

P.H.P. How was the chassis?

R.D. Very sound on this one. It was blasted and zinc plated, chassis blacked and the inside is filled with Waxoyl. All the body box sections are filled with oil.

P.H.P. And which model do you prefer?

R.D. Oh, the 140 definitely. It is so much nicer to drive.

Vic Gill who is on his fifth XK, acquired his 120 three years ago. When asked what he likes about the car, he simply replies, "everything"! The engine was seized when he bought the car, but he filled it up with Redex, turned it on the crank and he has not had to touch it since! The car is a very early steel bodied one, chassis number 610133, first registered in September, 1950. It has won several concours prizes and is the XK 120 featured in these pages.

P.H.P. How do you compare the various XKs, do you prefer the 120?

V.G. Yes, I do by far. Heavy steering doesn't bother me, to me it's part of the character. It's a personal thing and for me it's a combination of looks and driving. I have had 140s but I am a 120 man and I think the Roadster, being the first, is the classic one.

So there we are – complete disagreement! But I cannot help feeling that this is an excellent thing and part of the strength of the XK Register. Both 120s and

140s have a very special character of their own and long may we have enthusiasts who will argue for one or the other. And we must not forget those excellent XK150s

with their disc brakes, but that is another subject!

BUYING

Purchasing an XK can be a dangerous occupation. A bad decision can lead to a great deal of frustration and distress. The number of half-finished projects is testimony to the problems. However, I am not trying to dissuade anyone from owning an XK. In good condition they will give you tremendous pleasure, but you must be very careful in your choice and fully aware of the problem areas and costs of rectification. It is vital you know exactly what you are letting yourself in for.

Your first decision must, of course, be which model. This may be dictated by considerations of cost or particular affection for one model. Some are rarer than others. As a generalisation, because they are all similar mechanically and in construction, the problems are common to all.

Your major decision will be whether to buy a restored, part-restored, seemingly good original or a poor unrestored example. What are the considerations with each?

You should be very wary of a restored or good original car because XKs can quite skilfully hide their true condition. Most cars, however good they look,

have some corrosion in their bodies and repairing some corrosion usually means a total rebuild. A few tell-tale signs, on which I will elaborate later, indicate extensive rot. Do not forget that you cannot attach new good metal to old bad. So once you have started there is no stopping.

A less than reputable vendor can easily tart a car up with loads of filler and a reasonable paint job. How can you be sure there is no corrosion in the unseen box sections? Ideally I would always suggest removing the rear wings, though I am sure very few vendors would appreciate the suggestion. Unless the tonneau panels, or at least their edges, the inner wings and the outer wings have been replaced, and properly, I can almost guarantee that the appearance under there would remind you of a string vest.

So with a "good" car you are taking a risk unless the seller has photographs to prove what work has been done and you can see it has been done properly, or that he can prove to you by means of invoices that the restoration has been carried out by a reputable specialist, of whom there are very few.

What of a part-restored car? This will usually be a half completed project for which the seller has run out of enthusiasm or funds. Be very wary because often the work will not be up to standard and will have to be done again. Furthermore the project may be incomplete. It is obviously more difficult to tell whether all the parts are there when most are in boxes, and if you do not know the car well you may struggle to build it up, not having stripped it yourself.

So we come to the "heap" that looks dreadful and very clearly needs a major restoration. Paradoxically this is probably the best buy, providing you realise what you are letting yourself in for. As I have explained, even on

an apparently good car you will have to replace or repair most of the panels. Therefore the heap will be little different, except that you will pay a very much lower price for the horror.

Restoration is lengthy, expensive and difficult. These are realities that must be faced, but equally if you want a car to keep, that you can know is sound, it is the only way. The only qualification I would make to the "good" versus "horror" thinking is that the horror should be reasonably complete and preferably have its original engine.

So far I have concentrated on bodywork because it is the area in which XKs suffer most and is probably the most difficult area to restore. Indeed many firms and so-called specialists have found to their cost that XK bodies are extremely difficult to restore.

Getting down to detail the areas on the bodywork to inspect for tell-tale signs are as follows:

Bodywork

Front wings: The front sidelight housings (except the separate chrome sidelights fitted to early 120 Roadsters). These are a small pressed panel welded to the wing and leaded around. A slight ridge shows that the flange is lifting. A small bubble or two means corrosion is present. They are a natural moisture trap and any signs, however small, will indicate that the whole section will have to be cut out and replaced.

The headlamp nacelles. Like the sidelights, these are a separate pressing and under the nacelle there is often lifting evident.

The wing side behind the wheelarch. This has invariably been damaged and filled. Try running both hands simultaneously along the inside and outside of the panel to ascertain whether the thickness is constant. The vent box is a good haven for rust.

The front bottom area. As above.

The battery boxes (140 only). Situated inside the front wing(s), these rust badly, but are not too difficult to replace.

The wired edge. This area traps moisture and harbours rust. Look for surface rust on the edge and bubbles in the paintwork.

Rear wings:

General. Check for filler.

Top of wing. Any bubbles or lumps, however small, denote major work. Run your fingers along the wing front-to-rear and feel the profile. The wing piping should have been painted separately, and not be gummed up with paint or filler. The vertical panel above the wing on F.H.C. and D.H.C. models should also be carefully checked. The D.H.C. has the additional problem of the wooden hood mounting section which runs around the rear of the cockpit and retains moisture.

Front of the wing and "B" post. The front of the wing should be looked at carefully and similarly the shut face panel. Behind this is a box section called the shut face pillar. This is a suspect area. When badly rotted the whole "B" post section will move in and out, especially when closing the heavy doors.

Tonneau panels. These are the panels between the rear wing and the bootlid. They should be checked just above the wing piping from front to back.

Roof (F.H.C): Check guttering area.

Boot area: The boot floors where the spare wheel sits should be examined. Water can collect here and often you can see daylight where you should not! Look at the seams and corners.

Sills. These are visible with door open and connect "A" and "B" posts. They often corrode badly, particularly where they join the "A" and "B" posts.

"A" posts: The doors being,

on most models, extremely heavy and the hinges having no means of being lubricated can lead to door drop. Check by lifting door at open end. Replacing the hinge boxes is a major job and can involve cutting the outer wing. Look for evidence of bodged repairs in this area.

Doors: Check bottoms for bulging and paint flaking. Blocked drain holes can wreak havoc. Check tops along door-to-glass area for bubbles.

General: Stand at the rear of the car and look down the sides. The front wing, door and rear wing should be flat and not remind you of rolling hills. Similarly, mentally place a straight edge along the bottom line of the same three panels. There should be no steps up or down, or gentle curvature. Again look at the top line. There should be no steps and the general curvature should be consistent.

Chassis

The chassis are extremely strong but due to advancing years even XK chassis should be carefully examined for corrosion. Generally the area around the engine, which will have benefitted from the oily atmosphere, will be O.K. The area most prone to problems is at the rear where the chassis curves up and over the back axle. This is an important area because the spring hangers are attached to this section. One should also check the chassis at the front because I have known rot to be present here as well.

For mechanical advice I spoke to Harry Phillips of Phillips

Garage, Birmingham. He has been a Jaguar specialist for very many years and he has wide experience of the problems associated with XKs.

Engine

Oil pressure should be in excess of 40 lbs at 3000 rpm. Obviously listen for knocks and rattles, look for oil leaks (particularly from the rear crankshaft seal) and beware a smokey exhaust.

HP: "The most common thing is crank wear. If the rear main is leaking, that is a complete engine strip. But everything is obtainable. Listen for noisy timing chains. Basically though very straight-forward with no problems on parts."

Brakes

HP: "For XKs generally the biggest mechanical problem is the brakes, obtaining materials."

Steering

HP: "Steering is not so bad. All the balljoints have now been reproduced and we can recondition the racks."

Gearboxes

HP: "We cannot get gearbox parts these days. We have to have them made. The synchros are the big headache. We have to get the gears re-brassed and re-machined, and that can be costly."

Back Axle

HP: "They go on forever and a day. At worst it is just a question of changing bearings."

Suspension

Check for play and listen for clonks.

Interior Trim

Check for originality including leather seats rather than vinyl which is sometimes used for economy but will detract from the value. Providing they are not torn or too shabby, seats with a used look can often be more in keeping than brand new retrimmed seats. Retrims are very expensive today and the Drophead hoods particularly so.

Exterior trim

At the time of writing it is vital that "your" XK has such items as the chrome window trims and bonnet strips (140 only). These are not being remanufactured yet, whereas the majority of the other items like door handles, boot trim, lights, rubbers are available, though not cheap. In passing if you think these items are unjustifiably expensive spare a thought for the specialist who has had the nerve to invest hundreds or maybe thousands of pounds in tooling and stock to sell a small quantity per year.

I have tended to gloss over the mechanical details rather as these are less specialised and mechanical repairs are comparatively easy. I cannot overstress that it is bodywork that is the most perilous area with XKs.

To overcome the problems we are in the happy situation of having all minor and major panels available today. Though I do not, as yet, have any experience of using one, the low cost MIG welders obviously take a great deal of the skill out of welding thin metal where the avoidance of distortion with conventional gas welding is a highly skilled art. Nevertheless the XK body is not easy to build. As witness to that just see how many XKs meet the criteria I outlined above with regard to straight flat sides and correct bottom and top lines, with correct door gaps as well, of course.

Personally I would always advise replacing complete panels, such as front wings, rather than repair. The initial cost may seem high, but when you consider that the existing wing will very likely need new sidelight sections, repairs to the headlamp nacelles and lower front section, attention and possible replacement of the wired edge and replacement of the flat section behind the wheelarch, you will see that not very much is left untouched. Furthermore new metal must always be preferable to repairs.

One or two companies now make complete rear end sections and indeed complete bodies. Unless you are very experienced in panel beating and welding, I would recommend certainly fitting a complete rear end. It may seem an expensive way of doing it, but in the long run it will save a good deal of time and considerable hassle.

If you are having the work done for you, my advice is always, but always, use a well established specialist. You may be lucky to chance upon a local firm that will make a satisfactory job, but I can assure you you will be playing Russian roulette. The specialist will be familiar with the problems, will have stock or know sources and is not learning on your car. Anyone else is learning and the cost to you will either be inferior work, protracted legal battles or spiralling bills.

Even specialists are human and you must be prepared for costs to considerably exceed their estimates or your most pessimistic ones. Good communication is vital and visit the chosen workshop and maintain a regular dialogue to avoid misunderstandings. Unless you are convinvced you are being conned, try to put yourself in the shoes of the restorer and understand the problems he is having to cope with on your behalf. Restoration businesses are very difficult to run. I speak from experience!

The final advice I would give if you are thinking of acquiring an XK and enjoying the unique joys of XK motoring is to seek out local enthusiasts and glean all the advice you can from them. The chances are that they will have made a few mistakes as we all do in learning and most will be pleased to help you avoid the same mistakes. They will have found good firms and bad firms, and their advice could save you a lot of time and money.

The XK Register of the Jaguar Drivers' Club has monthly meetings all over the U.K. and at these you will meet the real enthusiasts. A visit to the annual International XK Day will enable you to compare all the various models and the parts available from a selection of the specialists.

Values

Finally turning to values, it is obviously pointless to quote actual figures as these vary from time to time. As everyone knows, with the advent of the E-type, XK prices dropped like a brick and in the sixties and very early seventies, one could acquire XKs for hundreds of pounds. Equally well known is the fact that in the mid and later seventies, XK prices shot up and were priced once again in thousands. Things began to steady out in the early eighties, but now in the mid-eighties values are again appreciating.

We tend to think of XKs as being expensive now, but I feel this is for two reasons. Firstly, we have known them cheap and so they are comparatively costly and secondly, they are now bought as additional 'fun' cars rather than everyday cars. It is my contention that in comparison with modern cars, whether they be Fords or Jaguars, XKs are still good value.

One must look at these things in what the economists call 'real' terms. Apparently average earnings rose 443% between 1971 and 1985, and the average price of a house increased from £5,650 to £30,000.

At one time 120s were considered far more desirable and consequently were far more expensive than 140s. This seems to have changed and there is rather less difference in the values these days. Similarly Roadsters were much more valuable than Dropheads and particularly Fixed Heads. Today there seems to be less differentiation.

The most encouraging thing about the mid-eighties' rise in values is that it has again become a viable exercise to restore XKs in financial terms. When a good car was worth, say, £10,000 and it was costing maybe £15,000 to purchase a heap and restore the car, it discouraged people or lead to less than satisfactory cheaper jobs.

I would guess that very few of us own XKs as a way of making money, but it is very encouraging to know that you should be able to have a lot of fun and, if necessary, get your money back. In comparison with modern cars, which seem to become increasingly boring, XKs are very good value. I think this will soon be realised and they will continue escalating in price. Now is the time to buy one!

CLUBS, SPECIALISTS & BOOKS

Clubs

Membership of a club, as mentioned previously, is essential. The XK Register of the Jaguar Drivers' Club was for many years the driving force within the Club. Today there are other excellent sections, such as the E-type Register, which are equally dynamic.

Many years ago members of the XK Register formed Area Meetings around the country, and even abroad for there are many Register members in Europe, the States, Australia and indeed all corners of the world. These Area Meetings have broadened out to encompass the whole club and are undoubtedly the strength of the J.D.C. The hierarchy of the Club has sadly been through turbulent times in the early eighties, but whoever is running its sections such as the XK Register will surely always survive and true enthusiasts have little time for politics.

The J.D.C. is lucky to enjoy the approval and friendship of Jaguar Cars whose collection, incidentally, includes a very original XK 120 Roadster and the ex-Ian Appleyard car, NUB 120.

Since the demise of the XK Club many years ago, the J.D.C. has had no rivals in the U.K., until the formation of the Jaguar Enthusiasts Club in the mid-eighties. Competition can only be healthy and will hopefully spur both clubs to greater things.

At the time of writing, it is believed the J.D.C. will shortly be moving its offices to Coventry. There is, therefore, little point in giving what will be the old address.

The Secretary of the XK Register is:
John Bridcutt Esq.,
The Post Office,
Market Lavington,
Nr. Devizes,
Wiltshire.

The address of the J.E.C. is:
Jaguar Enthusiasts' Club Ltd.,
FREEPOST,
Aldershot,
Hants GU12 5BR.

There are Jaguar Clubs in most countries around the World, with a number in the States.

Specialists

There are these days a great many so-called Jaguar specialists, but they come and go and one should be very wary who one deals with. I believe there is no substitute for specialisation and above all experience. The following list is by no means complete and there are, I am sure, many other reputable companies. I have selected those firms who are actually known to me or who have been around a long time and about whom I have only heard good reports. However no-one is perfect all the time and it is essential to go into these things with one's eyes well and truly open. Remember Jaguar work is very expensive and there are no short cuts. Equally a good XK will give tremendous pleasure.

Classic Autos
10, High Street,
Kings Langley,
Herts.
Proprietor – Aubrey Finburgh
Tel: Kings Langley (09277) 62994
Restoration, panelwork, parts. Aubrey has been involved in XKs longer than almost anybody.

Classic Power Units,
Tile Hill,
18, Trevor Close,
Coventry.
Proprietor – George Hodge
Tel: Coventry (0203) 461136
Engine rebuilds.

D.K. Engineering,
10/16, Hallwell Road,
Northwood,
Middx.
Proprietor – David Cottingham
Tel: Northwood (09274) 21399
Restoration and Sales.

Coventry Auto Components,
Gillingwood,
Waste Lane,
Berkeswell,
Nr. Coventry,
Warwickshire.
Proprietor – Trevor Scott – Worthington
Tel: Coventry (0203) 464644
Stockists and remanufacturers of parts including chromework, rubbers, brake parts, etc. Very helpful.

Alan R, George,
Plot 11,
Small Firms Compound,
Dodwells Bridge Ind. Est.,
Hinckley,
Leicester.
Proprietor – Alan George
Tel: Hinckley (0455) 615937
Manual and Automatic Transmissions.

Bill Lawrence,
9, Badgers Walk,
Dibden Purlieu,
Hampshire.
Proprietor – Bill Lawrence
Tel: Hythe (0703) 846768
Panel Manufacture (except
wings).
Bill Lawrence has specialized
in making just XK panels for
many years and has many
satisfied customers around
the world.

Marina Garage Ltd.,
Marina Close,
Sea Road,
Boscombe,
Bournemouth BH5 1BH
Proprietor (specializing in
restoration) – Bob Davis
Restoration, mechanical work
and servicing.

Phillips Garage,
206, Bradford Street,
Deritend,
Birmingham B12 ORG
Proprietor – Harry Phillips
Tel: 021 772 2000
All mechanical work, engine
rebuilds, exchange engines.
Long established and very
helpful.

R.S. Panels,
Kelsey Close,
Attleborough Fields Ind. Est.,
Nuneaton CV11 6RS,
Proprietor – Bob Smith
Tel: Nuneaton (0203)
388572/89561
Body restoration and
manufacture of front
and rear wings.
Not cheap, but first class
work.

Suffolk & Turley,
Unit 7,
Attleborough Fields Ind. Est.,
Garrett Street,
Nuneaton,
Warwickshire,
Proprietors – E. Suffolk &
M. Turley
Tel: Nuneaton (0203) 381429
Complete interior restorations,
ex-factory craftsmen.

Both cars featured in this
book were retrimmed by
this firm.

Southern Classics Ltd,
M.W.G. House,
Hanworth Lane,
Chertsey,
Surrey KT16 9LA
Proprietor – Alan Holdaway
Tel: Chertsey (09328) 67671
Restoration.

Swallow Engineering,
6, Gibcracks,
Basildon,
Essex,
Proprietor – Nick Smith
Tel: Basildon (0268) 558418
Restoration

Books

The Jaguar enthusiast is not
starved when it comes to books
on the subject and there are often
excellent articles in magazines
such as Classic & Sportscar,
Thoroughbred & Classic Cars and
the many others.

No-one has yet written the
definitive XK history, but Paul
Skilleter's contributions to the
whole Jaguar subject have been
immense. His tome, 'Jaguar Sports
Cars', has not surprisingly a large
section devoted to XKs in great
detail. Paul has also written a very
useful smaller book devoted
entirely to XKs and entitled, 'The
Jaguar XKs'.

In lighter vein is Chris
Harvey's book, 'The Jaguar XK'.
Chris like all the authors is a great
Jaguar enthusiast.

Andrew Whyte has used the
benefit of many years working for
Jaguar to write a fascinating
account of the company itself in
his book, 'Jaguar, The History Of a
Great British Car'. His highly
detailed volume, 'Jaguar – Sports
Racing & Works Competition Cars
to 1953' obviously includes much
of interest to XK enthusiasts.

The Brooklands Books
compilations of reprinted road
tests and contemporary reports
make interesting reading and are
useful for reference.

An excellent comprehensive
history of the company and its
products, including XKs, is
'Jaguar' by Lord Montagu. The
book has been updated over the
years and is most readable and
informative.

From around the world and
covering cars in their respective
countries are: France – 'Jaguar, A
Tradition of Sports Cars' by
Bernard Viart and Michael Cognet;
Australia – 'Jaguar Under the
Southern Cross' by Les Hughes
and 'Jaguar XK in Australia' by
Elmgreen and McGrath.

My own offering, 'Jaguar –
The Complete Illustrated History'
covers XKs in some detail, has
period anecdotes and a large
number of contemporary
photographs not seen before.

The XK devotee is happily
spoilt for choice.

PHOTO GALLERY

1. Examples of three XK models in different states of disrepair. From left to right they are; an XK 140 Roadster, rather shabby now after considerable use in the last decade, an XK 120 Roadster, which has been extensively bodily and mechanically restored and awaits painting and trimming, and an XK 120 Fixed Head.

2. The condition today of the ex-rally 120 FHC, 669003, can only be described as sad, but it serves to show where XKs suffer and will be rebuilt, one day!

3. The 120 boot area and spare wheel tray suffer badly from corrosion and here we see that the tray has actually collapsed.

4. Looking into the spare wheel stowage area one can see that the chassis has virtually disintegrated. Most XKs will not be as bad as this, but require careful checking.

5. Footwell ventilators were fitted from 1951 and situated inside the front wing ahead of the "A" post. The vent box assembly is an obvious haven for corrosion.

6. One of the most tell-tale areas of corrosion is the moulded-in sidelights fitted on later 120s and all 140s. A few bubbles and evidence of lifting looks terrible once the paint is removed.

7. The shut face panel and the area behind known as the shut face pillar should be checked and the sills, one of the main mounting areas of the body to the chassis, inspected.

8. The panel above the front of the rear wing is one of the worst areas for rot and again a few small bubbles will be horrifying once the exterior paint is removed.

9

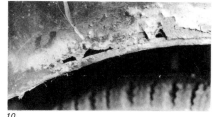

10

11

12

13

14

15

9. This photo of the 120 Roadster shows the outer wing removed and the inner wing and rear chassis leg visible. It is rarely sufficient to carry out minor localised repairs, but necessary to replace with new panels.

10. The bottom of the front wing and up over the wheel arch is finished off by rolling the metal over a length of wire. Dirt from the road collects in this wired edge, holds moisture and gradually corrodes through. Pinhead lumps in the paint indicate the area is porous.

11. With a front wing removed the construction of the "A" post and hinge boxes plus the battery boxes is evident. This is actually an XK 150, but is very similar to the 120 and 140, though only the latter had the battery boxes.

12. When inspecting an XK 140 with a view to purchase, always lift the rear carpets in the corner behind the seats and check the state of the floors for daylight or bodged repairs. The plywood floor extends to behind the seats on 120s.

13. The 140 has a well in which the spare wheel sits below the boot floor. Not surprisingly water collects in here. The seams, and lowest and forward-most corners rot away in much the same way as the 120.

14. Fixed Heads can be prone to rusting around the guttering area of the roof panel. One can also see here the problems around the wing seams that so many XKs suffer from. Everyone with experience of restoring XKs will tell you that once you have removed the paint even good looking cars can be almost as bad as this.

15. The classic lines of an early steel bodied XK 120 Super Sports complete with spats shows the simple, clean lines of one of Sir William's finest creations.

16. Bearing in mind that in the late forties and early fifties, there was effectively nothing on the road that could keep up with an XK anywhere in the world, this is presumably the view that became familiar to most motorists, and then only fleetingly.

16

17

18

19

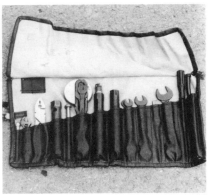

20

21

22

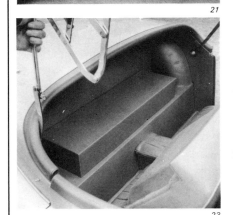

23

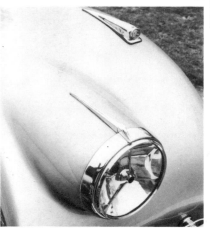

24

25

17. The 120 Open Two Seater dashboard was leather covered and sloped backwards whereas the Open 140 had a similar, but upright dash. The switch for the lights altered from 120 to 140.

18. The inside of a Roadster door shows the useful stowage pocket, the door opening cord which was the only means of opening the door as there was no exterior handle and the thumb screws for the side screens plus the door lock.

19. The Roadster hood was, to say the least, rudimentary and with the minute rear window and sidescreens in place, one can appreciate why so many commentators have referred to the claustrophobic effect.

20. This photograph shows a reproduction tool roll with original tools bar the later pliers.

21. This shot shows the sill, shut face panel, the rear spat which was fitted to all pressed steel wheeled cars, and the steering wheel with its distinctive, and rather dangerous, prominent horn push.

22. The Roadster, as the Open Two Seater was known in the States and has come to be known here, stowed its hood behind the rear seats and the hood sticks remained attached so that it could be swung out and up quite easily.

23. With the hood on its way up one can see the attachment points and the box cover under which were situated the two six volt batteries with which all 120s were fitted.

24. In this photograph can be seen the distinctive 120 'tripod' headlamps topped by a chrome headlamp spear and atop the wing the small chromed sidelight fitted to earlier Open cars. Like the rear lamps, they are bedded on a rubber gasket.

25. The 120 bootlid extended right to the bottom and carried a 'T' handle by which it was opened. The number plate was carried upon a raised plinth and the combined reversing/number plate lamp was perched above. The overriders gave little or no protection.

26

27

MDU 420

28

JAGUAR

29

26. An open bootlid reveals the luggage area and spare wheel compartment with jack stowed alongside. The fuel tank was situated ahead of the spare wheel.

27. A grab handle was thoughtfully provided for passengers and a small interior mirror situated behind the removable windscreen. The 120 driving position is a matter of individual taste with some taller drivers complaining of a lack of space.

28. Clark Gable was a keen Jaguar enthusiast and just one of many Americans who rushed to purchase the products from Coventry.

29. The XK 120 Fixed Head, introduced in March, 1951, had all the open car's performance with added sophistication, making it an ideal Grand Touring car in the true sense.

30. This XK 120 Fixed Head is probably an early car and differs in minor details from later ones but serves to show the high level of refinement.

31. The XK 120 Drophead Coupe, introduced in April, 1953, shared the same high level of interior appointment as the FHC but with the ability to lower its lined hood.

30

31

32

33

34

35

36

37

38

39

32. From a distance the most obvious difference between the old and new XKs is the extra chromework, especially the much criticized bumpers. Again pressed steel wheeled cars had spats whilst wire wheeled cars did not as the spinners protruded.

33. The sophisticated hood fitted to the Drophead Coupe resulted in a very civilised car when up and was very easily lowered making the 140 Drophead a very practical all round XK.

34. The 140 bootlid, which now carried a cast chromed strip, badge and plunger type handle, stopped just above the new bumper line and the number plate plinth was mounted to a separate fixed panel below.

35. The moulded-in sidelight was introduced on the XK 120 Fixed Head and later adopted for the Roadsters. They were retained for all the 140 models and the small red perspex 'tell-tale' on the top enabled the driver to see if the sidelights were working.

36. Pressed steel wheels were finished in body colour on all models and on 120s the hub caps had the indented sections body colour whereas on the 140s the whole hub cap was chromed. The background to the badge was black.

37. That the 140s rear bumpers and overriders were a much sturdier job than the 120s can clearly be seen. Jaguar did consider a complete one piece rear bumper, but mercifully decided on quarter bumpers only.

38. As opposed to its predecessor's cast item, the 140's rear lamps were pressed and contained a reflector as well as doubling as the rear indicators. Wing beading was always body colour.

39. The rear window could be unzipped on both 120 and 140 Dropheads. The hood, which was lined and beautifully made, was known as a 'wig top' because it followed the approximate lines of the closed version and is not surprisingly very expensive to replace today.

40

40. With the 140 bootlid raised one can immediately see further differences. The spare wheel now lives out of sight under a hinged wooden boot floor which is covered in Hardura. At the front of the luggage area the vertical panel hinged forward into the cockpit to allow golf clubs to be carried.

41. A hood bag was provided to neaten up the lowered hood and behind the main seats were situated the small occasional ones for the family man's offspring. Access was gained by tilting the front seats forward.

42. The XK's bonnet has been aptly likened to an alligator and did not greatly assist access to the engine which was a very tight fit as can be seen.

43. The dash of the Fixed and Drophead Coupe models positively oozed luxury and was closely based on the style of the saloons.

44. Driving an XK, one has the magnificent view down the long bonnet. Pre-war the SS and SS Jaguar bonnets were for show, but the XKs changed all that.

45. In profile the XK 140 Fixed Head looked quite different from the earlier model and was certainly a more practical machine for the family man with its additional interior space.

46. Many people consider the 140 FHC to be their favourite shape of all. It is my opinion that the car benefits in the looks department from the wire wheels and consequent lack of spats.

47. The XK 140 Roadster is a superb compromise. Barring the unfortunate bumpers, it has the classic lines of the original model yet enjoys the benefits of rack and pinion steering and a little more power.

41

42

43

44

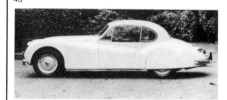

45

46

47

48

49

50

51

52

53

54

55

56

57

58

48. The late Peter Walker in number 27 and Duncan Hamilton, two great Jaguar racing names, engage in a fine tussle during the 1951 Production car race at Silverstone.

49. The XK 120 driven by Nick Haines and Peter Clark finished a highly creditable 12th in the 1950 Le Mans 24 Hour Race and this performance and that of the other two XKs, persuaded Jaguar to return with specially designed competition cars.

50. This car, the second Fixed Head built, was driven by Johnson, Hadley, Fairman and Moss for seven days and nights achieving an average of more than 100 mph.

51. The next right-hand drive Fixed Head to be built and the first to be released was this car seen during its rallying career. Is is the same car as the restoration project shown earlier!

52. The author's 120 Roadster seen in the first photo in this secton was also used in rallying as were a number of early cars.

53, 54, 55. One of the most active and widely used XKs in rallying was the 120 belonging to Midlands businessman, Frank Grounds. These shots show him competing in two R.A.C. Rallies and the Tulip Rally. The car later gained a home-made fixed head body and has recently resurfaced. It is now being rebuilt.

56. Another extensively campaigned Open Two Seater was that of Bertie Bradnack seen here taking part in the British R.A.C. Rally in close company with another 120.

57. Chief Tester, and a stalwart member of the small distinguished team that designed and developed all the competition and production Jaguars, Norman Dewis achieved no less than 172 mph and in this XK 120.

58. The XK 140s were not entered in competitive events to the same degree as 120s, but when they were, they gave a very respectable account of themselves. An example was the 140 FHC of Bolton and Walshaw which only cruel luck prevented from finishing well at Le Mans in 1956.